ReBoot

My Five Life-Changing Mistakes
...and How I Moved On

JULIE WAINWRIGHT

WITH ANGELA MOHAN, M.F.T.

Designed by kenCREATIVE, www.kenCREATIVE.com.

For information regarding special bulk discounts email:
Feedback@smartnow.com.

ISBN: 1-4392-3255-5
EAN: 97814392325

For Lisa, Sherry and Jim,
Thank you for being wonderfully real, silly and loving.

For Dad,
Your love carries me. Your integrity and spirit inspire me.

To my amazing friends, Kenny and Mitch,
You have always been lights in my life. Thank you for believing in me
when I didn't believe in myself.

For Mark,
Thank you for showing me how to love again.

For Tyson,
Your big heart saved my heart from shrinking.

For all who emailed me and left posts under the original blog,
You inspire me. Thank you.

For all artists,
Your courage and dedication to expression helped me transcend
my darkness. I honor and salute you.

This book is also dedicated in memoriam to my mother,
Sandy, whose empathy towards all is imbedded in my cells.

Contents

INTRODUCTION

What would you do if your wings failed you? If you are like me, you would simply flap harder, only to crash, wondering all the way down if you were Icarus.

This is my story of a very public crash, followed by a meltdown, followed by something totally unimaginable. This book began as a blog I thought a handful of people would read. In less than a year's time, nearly 100,000 people had read "The Five Mistakes" blog in over 156 different countries. I have also received hundreds of emails from readers, many asking me for more information, and others requesting the blog in book form so they could give it as a gift. I am so humbled.

Thank you. This book is for you. And if it has a positive effect on you, please share it with others.

BEFORE PETS.COM

I am the product of artists. My parents met as students at the Chicago Art Institute and I was born within 12 months of their marriage, one year after my father graduated and my mother dropped out of school to be his bride. (Don't worry; I'm not going to walk you through every year until now. This is the Cliffs Notes version of a life.)

My mother had four children before she turned 29. The birth of her fourth child brought with it an unexpected consequence: illness. I remember our very first family meeting vividly. I was eight, my sister, Lisa was four, my brother Jim was two, and a neighbor held the youngest, my sister Sherry, who was just three months old. We were sitting on the couch, huddled together and my father stood in front of us with a grave look on his face. I had my arm around Lisa and held her tightly to my side, probably to torment her a little, but mainly out of fear. Something was up and I knew it wasn't good. Our mother had been in the hospital for a while and I didn't understand what was happening and why I wasn't allowed to see her. Finally, my father started to talk. Our mom was probably going to die and while there was a chance she might come home again, he wasn't hopeful.

He said that she had something called encephalitis. Even though I was just 8 and barely able to comprehend his words, this disease seemed unlikely to me. We were told her brain was swelling due to a mosquito bite. I remember asking my father how she could have been bitten by a mosquito when it was bitter cold with snow on the ground. I don't remember his answer, but I know it didn't satisfy me. I knew enough to realize that our hometown, South Bend, Indiana, a place of sub-zero winters and Notre Dame, didn't have mosquitoes in January, the month she was supposedly infected.

I was right. Our mother didn't have encephalitis and she didn't die. She returned home within a few weeks to resume her life as the mom of four chaotic children. Unfortunately, she didn't get well either. Her health continued to fail in mysterious ways that puzzled her and her doctors for years, until one day her right side completely collapsed. The doctors ran several tests, including a painful spinal tap and finally, the mystery was solved, summed up in two small but terrifying words: multiple sclerosis. She was in and out of hospitals for the rest of her life.

After that first momentous family meeting, I felt like it was my job to be the mom. I'm not sure if my dad asked for my help or I just instinctively knew he needed it. Whatever the case, I took my little mom role seriously, both when my mother was ill and even when she wasn't. I became a whiz at helping out and taking responsibility.

Her illness shaped my character in other ways, too. I, along with entire family, developed a warped sense of humor. We found it impossible to live in emotional pain all the time, so we began to find the humor in the oddest things. Laughter was medicinal and we took our medicine wherever we could find it, constantly searching for opportunities amid bleak situations.

Here's an example of what I mean: since my mother was sick regularly and since I grew up in the Midwest, our neighbors filled the gaps her illness left. They always knew what was happening in our house and their preferred method of caretaking was food, especially dinner, which was delivered piping hot in Corning glass dishes. Those dinners consisted mostly of casseroles — the two most common were tuna-mushroom casserole with canned fried onions sprinkled on the top and hamburger casserole made with Hamburger Helper. There were some casseroles whose identities were unknown, but I guarantee you, they all had noodles and canned creamy soup in them. Everyone was very generous with food, but they weren't all great cooks.

This presented a problem. We needed a way to weed the good casserole makers from the bad ones. Since I was a natural problem-solver, I decided that this called for a rating system, one that we could easily reference. I developed a hand-drawn grid with each neighbor's name, the last delivered meal and an A if it was good or an F, if it wasn't. Our family wasn't much for the middle — either you delivered something yummy or your meal went into the trash compactor. Here's the way I remember the system working: the phone would ring, and Mrs. K. would ask if we needed any food. I'd ask her to hold for a moment, while I pretended to check with my dad (or the housekeeper if my mom was in the hospital), and I'd rush to the cabinet and check the grid. I was the food gatekeeper, but we all contributed to the rating system. If the meals were a consistent A, we were "really hungry" and if the neighbor had a high propensity of Fs, well, the freezer was stocked, but "thanks so much for asking". We also got lots of desserts. Those were on the grid, too, but it was a fairly sure bet that if the meal was an F, so was dessert. Lucky for us, we had more A cooks in the neighborhood than Fs. We all ate very well during my mom's downtimes and took glee in the rating system.

Then there was the time when our mom was going through experimental radiation treatment combined with ste-roids. She turned red and puffy and developed acne. Since I was a teenager, we shared acne medicine, and I referred to her as my tomato, which she thought was so funny she laughed until she cried.

And that's how it went for most of my years at home. I was a pseudo mom with lots to think about and a young girl with all of the awkwardness that brings. By the time I turned 18, I was so adept at juggling my problem-solving-mom persona with my student life, I graduated from high school with top honors. Needless to say, I was a little chubby because of all of those casseroles.

Ever the over-achiever, I was off to Purdue to study pharmacy. After the first year I couldn't imagine doing that for living and began searching for a new major. I took more art classes and kept over thinking the art. I took more science classes, but I was empty creatively. As luck would have it, I happened to be doing my boyfriend's marketing homework and discovered that I loved it. He got great grades on the papers I did for him. I promptly changed my major to business with an emphasis in marketing. I was soon hooked on business. It provided a uniquely cool balance of math, logic and creativity.

Keeping with my Type-A behavior (and because I needed to help out with college expenses), I worked my way through college doing lots of different jobs. For the record, my three favorites were: being Mrs. Santa Claus (although it was only a seasonal gig, it sure was fun); a department story window designer-in-training (I loved learning from a top window designer who had settled in Lafayette, Indiana from New York City, an odd choice for him, but great for our local department store's windows — and me); and a riveter on the Monte Carlo rear bumper assembly line at a General Motors plant in Anderson, Indiana. In my riveter role, I sat across the bumper line from Sadie, a red-haired woman who always wore her hair in a beehive, had metallic turquoise eye shadow that swooped up to her brow line, wore tight white three-piece polyester suits to work (I think she was after the foreman), showed ample cleavage and talked about sex with her boyfriend who she said looked like Burt Reynolds. Once she asked me what I thought of her sex talk and I replied, "You are a wanton woman, Sadie." To which she shot back, "I'm not wantin' anything after this last weekend." Now, she was some education.

I graduated Purdue cum laude and managed to impress my consumer psychology professor so much that he called The Clorox Company and told them they should hire me. I started at Clorox in brand management shortly after that gracious call. I was only the second undergraduate Clorox had ever hired.

Clorox was what I imagine boot camp is. All new brand management hires worked 12-14 hour days, mostly number-crunching and analyzing trends. This was before the personal computer, so we became very proficient in running the classic "what if" scenarios by hand: what if the price of trucking liquid bleach goes up by $150 a truck load, can that increase be absorbed in the price and what will happen in key competitive markets? What if private labels drop their price below 49 cents per quart; how will that erode our quart market share, distribution and line profitability? I'm sure you get the idea. The young recruits were bombarded with endless numbers and requests for analysis on possibilities and trend projections which we all did on TI calculators over and over again.

Then one day, Jim, from the finance department, called me down to his office to show me the Apple computer he'd smuggled into the department. He pressed a few buttons and presto! What used to take me days of hand-computing was done instantly in his spreadsheet program. I'm not kidding you, I cried. It was remarkable. I knew I wanted to be part of this industry, and when I got a call from the wife of a former boss asking me to join a new personal computer software start-up, Software Publishing Corporation, I jumped at the chance. I resigned from Clorox as soon as I had the offer in writing. Before I could leave, however, I had to have my exit interview.

Clorox insisted that all exit interviews happen with the General Manager of the division. The GM of the bleach division was extremely intimidating. Just looking at him made me stutter. I visibly shook as I walked into his office and took my seat across from him at his wide desk. I'm pretty sure you could have landed a small airplane on that desk. He emphatically told me that he could generate more revenue by raising the price of bleach by one cent than the entire personal computer industry was generating. He was right, but I didn't care. I was young and excited about the possibilities that I knew personal computers would bring. I believe I told him that verbatim, although I'm sure I sputtered as I said the words.

I joined Software Publishing Corporation, one of the first personal computer software companies, a few weeks later. I was just 25. That was my entrée into the compelling world of technology. Within a couple of years, the company sent me overseas to live and run International sales and marketing, which broadened my life and horizons in ways I never dreamed. I moved to London in 1984. I traveled the planet with that job, meeting people all over the world who were just as enthusiastic about the personal computer revolution. It wasn't about the money or riches it could bring then; it was an industry that was changing lives and empowering people. Fine, maybe that is the innocence of youth talking. I'm sure it was about getting rich for some, but I didn't see it that way, nor do I remember that attitude from anyone else.

I lived in London twice during my International sales and marketing days. The second time from 1990-1993, brought my future husband, David, into my life. I was throwing a party and he came along with some very dear friends of mine. His kind eyes mesmerized me that night and his melodic voice closed the deal. We married at the Kensington Chelsea Town Hall about nine months after our first kiss, and, boy, did we think we had our lives together. Ah, love.

David and I returned to the States to live in California and I eventually joined Berkeley Systems, a software company known for its flying toaster screensaver software. I was quickly promoted to President and then CEO, because the company's revenue was nose-diving and the Board of Directors needed a plan. I had that plan. Nothing like a dire situation to give someone an opportunity. Hard work combined with a dose of luck and the help of some great people enabled me to success-fully turn the company around. The luck? I had the opportunity to guide the ship when it launched one of the most successful games of all time, You Don't Know Jack. It bucked the trends of the popular shooter games in the market eventually selling nearly 10 Million units and was named game of the year by the hard-core gamers. That was thrilling and downright fun. The success of You Don't Know Jack prompted the founder to sell the company. After Berkeley Systems was sold, I once again started knocking on doors to get a new job, this time as CEO.

E-commerce, at that point an exciting new way to shop, was just beginning to make a dent in people's conscious-ness. I was energized by the possibilities of using the Internet to purchase practically anything. Amazon.com had already proven that is was a super way to shop, so when I was offered the position of CEO in a hot new start-up that sold movies over the Internet, Reel.com, I jumped at the opportunity.

As it goes with life, on the heels of accepting the offer to join Reel.com, I got one of those calls — my mom was back in the hospital and it didn't look good. I arrived at the hospital late on a Friday afternoon. My poor little tomato was down to about 80 pounds of twisted bones. Her brain was frazzled with dementia and she was terrified because she didn't know where she was (a hospital) or why she was there (she was dying) or who we were (her family) or why we were dressed the way we were (in masks and gloves because she was quarantined due to a very serious infection, MRSA, that is generally considered antibiotic resistant and is highly contagious). She also had pneumonia, a urinary tract infection and really bad breath. That's right, bad breath. (I did mention I can find the humor in everything, didn't I?) Oxygen tubes were jammed up her nostrils. One arm was constrained to allow antibiotics and pain medicine to flow through her tiny dot of a body. Her skin was yellow and waxy.

If you remove the MRSA part of the above description, it was actually a pretty familiar scene. Our family had been on 'death watch' for nearly 2 years. It was a tragically familiar cycle: the call would generally come in the morning. My siblings and I would then get on planes, trains or in automobiles and make our way to the hospital where we'd camp out with her as she struggled to stay alive. She'd recover, occasionally recognize one or all of us and then take the ambulance back to the nursing home. There she would spend a few days, or even a month or two buzzing around the nursing home hallways in her wheelchair, only to get sick again. Every sickness took a little more out of her and each time, she became more and more physically compromised, but she did not die. We almost started to take her ability to skirt death for granted, since she always found the strength to rebound. Consequently, we all stopped going to the hospital for every emergency.

This time did feel different, though. It seemed impossible for her to survive the overwhelming number of complications that besieged her body. The MRSA alone was too powerful for her to overcome and truth be told, I wanted her to escape her withered, tired body and find some peace. We took shifts by her bedside so she wouldn't be alone. Three days crawled by minute-by-minute. Her breath halted and returned, time and time again. Then she opened her eyes, said she was hungry, looked around and politely said hello to each of us as she forced her body upright.

About an hour passed and mom chatted with each of us. She remembered things about her grandchildren we didn't think she knew due to her dementia.

(A short note here: our mother had dementia for years before she died. Our experience with her in this state was one of constant mystery. It was as if there was some part of her brain that could access memories, or "files", randomly, but vividly. Every once in a while, she accessed a good file, lucidity returned and brought with it hope. We would almost start to believe that her personality and memory were back, only to have the reality thrust in our faces when, in a split second, she would ask a question like what we were wearing to the prom. No matter how many times we went through it, the brief moment of hope followed by despair and realization of her illness was devastating.)

That day we had our old mom back with us. She was aware of real events that had happened in the recent past. She had real discussions about real people. Then, without warning, she slid back down, closed her eyes and seemed to fall asleep.

Her breathing labored. She cried out in pain. Tears streamed down her cheeks. We kept asking the nurse to give her more morphine, but our pleas fell on deaf ears. Our mother was already at her legal daily morphine limit. Her breathing stopped. Her throat gurgled. We watched as her body turned ashen. She took another breath. This went on for hours. We stopped breathing when she stopped, waiting for some sign that it was her last breath. Then she would gasp for air and, as if on cue, we, too, would gasp for a breath.

Finally, her breath became so faint that we had to get closer to hear her. Her chest barely moved. Her body turned bluish instead of grayish. We couldn't hear a sound and we didn't see her move. After 20 minutes, we looked around the room. "She's dead", my brother said. "Dead, wow, this is how someone dies", I remember saying.

The room was eerily quiet and then my brother said, "She doesn't look comfortable" and he started playing with the bed controls, at one point adjusting the angle of the bed so aggressively, she was propelled across the bed. Her tiny MRSA-ridden body landed half-on and half-off the bed nearly touching the floor next to him. Horror-stricken, I screamed, "What are you doing? She's dead! She can't be uncomfortable. Put her back."

I should mention that we were advised not to have any skin-to-skin contact with her due to her MRSA. During our vigil, we all wore hospital gloves, but when we realized she was dead, we removed them and put them in the contamination container. Needless to say, my brother couldn't gently scoop up her little body, place her head on the pillow, close her eyes and daintily fold her hands across her chest. He could have been infected. So he used the tools he had. He corrected the bed in the same aggressive manner he moved it the first time, with one hard stomp on the bed's foot pedal. This time, she went flying in the opposite direction, toward me. I screamed as her body did a trampoline bounce and landed against the bed rail on the opposite side of the bed, just one little bounce away from my lap. I looked up and met the eyes of my brother and sisters. We all started laughing uncontrollably. It was like a bad episode of I Love Lucy.

Clearly, the nurse heard us, because she ran into the room, and saw my mother's face smashed into the bed rail, an arm and a leg dangling over the side of the bed and her torso twisted in a non-human v-shaped angle. The nurse surveyed the situation and of course, this only made us laugh harder. She asked us if this was our mother and we were barely able to utter "yes". Her follow-up question, "Is she dead?" was even funnier. The nurse made a hasty retreat and I remember thinking how gruesome this must have seemed. But she had to have seen this type of reaction before, right? Surely, we weren't that off. Were we?

That uncontrollable laughter was the only way we knew how to clear our heads. The horror of her death closed in and choked us in that smelly, MRSA-quarantined room. We cried later. She was just 62 when she died. I turned 42 the day before her death.

Immediately after her funeral, I started as CEO of Reel.com. The job was great, but the combination of my mother's death and this new position put a strain on my marriage. Looking back, my marriage had been in trouble before Reel.com. The relationship that worked for us in England wasn't working back here in the States and our differences became more apparent than our similarities.

I wondered why we had gotten married in the first place. We were just too different. I was, and still am in overdrive, constantly thinking I need to do more and be more. I never felt able to rely on anyone to pay my way. I'm sure this is deeply related to the instability of my mother's health, and the pressure I felt to care for my family at such a young age. David, on the other hand, is and was a more relaxed person who believed the Universe would provide. He was uncomfortable with the blatant capitalism he experienced in the U.S., and more at home with theories of psychological motivations, which served him as a therapist, but was in stark contrast to who I was and what I wanted from life.

I started to have the disturbing realization that I found more satisfaction in my cubicle than I did in my home while I was working at Reel.com. If that isn't bleak, I don't know what is. I artfully pushed this back into the recesses of my brain while I worked, which was mostly all of the time.

Reel.com was a great success for its investors and it was sold to Hollywood Entertainment within two years after I joined. It was also a good experience for me. And, most days, I also managed to hold onto the illusion of life being okay at home, too. Unfortunately, that illusion couldn't last. Pets.com, my next company, was the proverbial straw that broke the camel's back. And heart.

PETS.COM

I left Reel.com in February 1999 to build Pets.com. Pets.com's rise and fall has been chronicled way too many times to go over the story again here — and frankly, that requires an entire book. But I would like to say a few things about it. If I were to sum it up in one sentence, it would be: Pets.com was the most intense experience I have ever endured.

The press coverage was surreal. Pets.com regularly received press on all major news stations including CNN and ABC, all the major newspapers and all the major radio stations. Dotcoms were skyrocketing in stock market valuations, so they were a source of endless fascination. Plus, Pets.com was the first fully-funded e-commerce site that focused exclusively on the pet sector. And after we announced Pets.com's funding, seven more were funded in what seemed to be the blink of an eye. Now that is insane even by dotcom standards. The press had a field day with this. The best way to give you a feel for the press is to revisit some of the headlines. And, since most of the reporting was incorrect and incomplete, I'll start with the headline and then give you a glimpse into what was really going on in the company.

Here is the timeline:

MARCH 1999

San Francisco Business Times, March 12, 1999: "Fast-moving Web CEO Takes on New Pet Project"

The opening sentence in this article says, "Julie Wainwright's Internet career has gone to the dogs — not to mention cats, parakeets and goldfish." I give this interview before I even join the company. I am on vacation and just a few days out of Reel.com. Pets.com's future investors and I are so convinced that once we announce the formation and funding of Pets.com, the other potential pet competitors and their investors, will fold their tents and do something else. This doesn't happen.

At this point in the company's young life, everything has great potential.

Forbes.com, March 29, 1999: "Amazon Eyes Pet Supplies"

Forbes reported Amazon's investment in Pets.com, citing their ownership at 50% of the company. This is completely false. In truth, Amazon is a significant investor and shareholder. Once again, the investors in Pets.com and I think that Amazon investing in the company will result in other competitors exiting. That doesn't happen.

April 1999

PRNewswire, April 28, 1999: "Sold Out! Red Herring's Venture 99 Conference Attracts Industry Leaders."

I am a speaker at this conference along with headliners Mary Meeker of Morgan Stanley and Mike Volpi of Cisco. I drive to the conference at Lake Tahoe and I'm already so tired that I nearly drive off the side of the mountain road into a ravine. When I get there, the actor who plays Elaine's boss on

"Seinfeld" is hanging around the lobby with a hotshot entrepreneur who has hired him to add star power to his web venture. Wow. The Internet has arrived. Everyone I talk to thinks it's odd, yet kind of cool that an actor is here with the nerds.

MAY 1999

U.S.News & World Reports, May 17, 1999: "Tail of the Pampered Pooch"

This article sings the praises of the pet sector. It also states that Pets.com now has True Pet, Pogopet, Pet.net and AcmePet as competitors. The playing field is heating up. By the end of May Petopia.com, Petstore.com and Petsmart.com are also funded. Pets.com now has about thirty employees and we are subletting a portion of an office from a friend of mine, using our personal cell phones to recruit employees and conduct business since we have a neither a phone system, nor an office.

JUNE 1999

CNNmoney, June 14, 1999: "Amazon Gets A Pet"

This article reports Pets.com's new $50 Million investment from Amazon and HummerWinblad. Businessweek, Newsweek, USA Today, Associated Press, Wired and The Wall Street Journal all cover this story. Pets.com has raised $60 Million dollars at this point. Once again, we are sure the competition will run away yelping with their tails between their legs when they read this. I mean, come on, 50 MILLION DOLLARS?! OF NEW FUNDING?? They'd all be crazy to continue to compete with us.

They don't run away. Instead, yet another competitor is funded.

The Pets.com website hasn't even launched, but we do have an office on Brannan Street in San Francisco and about 60 employees.

JULY 1999

Forbes, July 5, 1999:
"Dog Fight"

Here's where it starts to get ugly. Forbes covers the companies funded in the Internet pet space. The title of the article says it all. Back home in Pets.com land, we focus on launching the site, scheduled for August.

For the first time, investment bankers visit us and ask when we expect to go public. We tell them we need to launch the site first.

August 1999

Pets.com launches. Ten days after Petopia. My phone starts ringing off the hook the day Petopia launches. My investors are not happy. We are late to market, late by ten days. Investment bankers approach us about going public. This time, we inform them that we do not have a projectable business model.

September 1999

VNU Business Media, September 3, 1999: "Pets.com Delivers Ad Message With Sock"

Sock Puppet commercials are running in four key markets, San Francisco, New York, Chicago and Los Angeles.

Our sales go up in each of those cities. People either love the puppet or hate it. We start to get mail from people asking us if we know the puppeteer's arm is visible in the commercial. We know. We're going for silliness.

For the third time, investment bankers approach us about going public. We reiterate that our business is not projectable.

OCTOBER 1999

Forbes, October 18, 1999:
"Dot-com Brand-building Runs Wild"

This article chronicles the rise in cost of prime-time network TV spots due to dotcom advertisers. Forbes reports that over 100 dotcoms have hired top advertising agencies to produce television and radio spots. Pets.com is cited in the article.

Investment bankers approach us about going public. We listen. We think we should prepare to go public.

November 1999

San Francisco Chronicle, November 4, 1999: "Net Pet Sites Vie for Bucks, Partnerships"

This article announces Petstore.com's $97 Million funding from Discovery Communications. By this time, Petopia.com had raised $66 Million. Within days, we announce that Pets.com has secured another $35 Million making our total capital raised, $100 Million. We are all worried that one of our competitors will beat us to an IPO and therefore, be able to buy market share more aggressively than we can.

We choose Merrill Lynch as our investment banker with the goal of a planned public offering in the first quarter of 2000.

The Sock Puppet is in The Macy's Thanksgiving Day Parade. Pets.com does not pay to be in the parade; the parade organizers want us (or The Sock Puppet anyway) so badly we don't have to pay. We think this is a very good sign and recognize that our little puppet is becoming quite the celebrity. Al Roker, one of the parade's hosts, yells out a line from the Pets.com commercial "I love stuffed things," as the Sock Puppet floats by his viewing stand. During a company meeting, I play a video recording of his reaction to the puppet and everyone cheers. Talk about building company morale. We love being loved.

DECEMBER 1999

San Francisco Business Times, December 17, 1999: "Pet e-tailer Pets.com files for $100M IPO"

Pets.com's business is booming. We all work in the warehouse at night to reduce back orders. We negotiate a deal with Petstore.com to acquire them. Turns out, they did not actually get $97 Million dollars in cash. Not even close. What they got was something much less in the form of free advertising from their investment partner, Discovery. A member of Discovery's executive team joins our board.

Disney makes a small investment in Pets.com. We revise our S-1, the document a corporation files with the SEC prior to an initial public offering, to reflect the investment from Disney and our merger with Petstore.com. We work every day except Christmas. On December 30th, we are notified by

Merrill Lynch that one of our competitors has contacted the CEO of Merrill Lynch and offered them millions of dollars now and in future business not to take us public. Phones ring late into the night. Our IPO might not happen. Finally, we hear that Merrill Lynch is staying with us.

January 2000

USA TODAY, January 27, 2000: "Pets.com To Put Puppet On Bowl Ad"

We decide to run an ad during Super Bowl XXXIV. The Pets.com website collapses the day of the game and goes back up just ten minutes before the ad runs. The ad drives so much traffic to the site it nearly crashes again. The day after the Super Bowl, USAToday declares the puppet the Super Bowl winner for Viewer's Favorite Ad.

I leave for the IPO road show. By the end of the month, our bankers tell us that the market is cooling towards all Internet IPO's. We put out a press release that says we have lowered our expected raise from the IPO from $100 Million to $80 Million.

FEBRUARY 2000

Wired, February 1, 2000:
"Women Geeks Honor Their Own."

Cnet News.com, February 11, 2000:
"Pets.com Lacks Bite On First Day Of Trading"

CNNMoney, February 11, 2000:
"Pets.com Flops On Wall Street"

Internetnews.com, February 11, 2000:
"Pets.com: For the IPO Litter Box?"

The New York Times, February 11, 2000:
"Pets.com Gets Lukewarm Reception on
Wall Street"

CNBC-Squawk Box, February 14, 2000:
"Pets.com Got a Lukewarm Reception on
Wall Street"

TheStreet.com, February 15, 2000:
"Bad IPO! Pets.com Doggie Flogged Despite
Lovable Branding Face"

CNBC Marketwrap Interview, February 18, 2000: "Is There Anyway To View This Deal Other Than Disappointing?"

February is an odd month. First, I receive an award for being one of the top women in technology along with pioneers Carol Bartz, Ann Winblad, Ellen Franklin and Donna Dubinsky. Next, I raise $80 Million in public capital — and Pets.com is considered a flop. Measuring against Internet IPOs in 1999, it is a flop. Kudos are so fleeting.

I realize that investors' negative sentiment transcends Pets.com. I believe all Internet companies are in for a rough ride going forward. So do Pets.com's bankers. I'm unable to speak to the market dynamics during any of my post IPO interviews. I firmly believe that Pets.com will be the last Internet IPO for a long time. I work with my management team to dramatically cut expenses. We schedule a management offsite to discuss managing in a down economy, in which access to capital is nonexistent. As a note, this is nearly one year prior to any dot-com crisis noted by the press.

And it didn't get better. Rather than drag you through

the next nine months of mostly negative press, I am hitting the fast forward button to the week I announce that Pets.com will be shut down. Here's how the beginning of that fateful week in November 2000 played out.

NOVEMBER 2000

Sunday, November 6, 2000: I'm restless and tired. My brain won't shut down. I have so much on my mind, including the upcoming call with the SEC and NASDAQ on Monday morning to verify shut-down announcements and procedures for suspension of trading on Tuesday, November 8th. Pets.com is setting a precedent of closing its doors with a net positive worth. This is unfathomable. Business professors will tell you this never happens; companies either succeed or go bankrupt. In my mind (and my Board of Director's) running the company into bankruptcy when we have a net positive worth now, but aren't profitable and believe that we can't raise further capital to get to profitability, is both unethical and unthinkable.

The day is ridiculously long and I go to bed very late. I can't sleep. I can't stay awake either. I'm in that suspension mode, like jet lag without the trip.

Monday, November 7, 2000: Today is a crazy day. Top executives leave for our warehouse in Greenwood, Indiana in preparation for the employee meeting there on Tuesday. Back in San Francisco, the Vice President of Human Resources is finalizing all termination notices and severance checks while organizing a job fair for terminated employees later in the week. I don't remember leaving work that day, but I do remember waking up the next morning in my own bed.

Tuesday, November 8, 2000: David whispers in my ear. It's roughly 4am. He asks me if I am awake. I am. I have been staring at the nothingness on my ceiling all night. I'm awake all right. He says, "I want out of our marriage. I am done." Inside my head, I think 'Wow, he is really showing initiative for the first time in ages. How about that? Well done, David, gold star for you. Too bad you picked the end of our marriage as the place to assert yourself.' What I say is "Let's talk about a plan for you to leave now. I don't want this lingering on if you want out. I can't take it. I'm not that strong." That was his exit interview. We agree to separate our lives just like that. Poof. Marriage gone.

I shower, do my hair and make-up, drive to work and walk into the office, where over 100 employees (and one reporter who snuck into the office) gather to hear what I have to say. I cry as I discuss the closure. I apologize to them. I discuss the details of their severance and what will happen the rest of the week. Employees cry. They applaud me (talk about generous spirits!). I scream at the reporter once she is identified in the crowd. I keep screaming at her as I leave the meeting and with the help of one particular employee, a really big guy, escort our perpetrator reporter to the door. I keep screaming at her even after she is out the door. I tell her I will have her arrested if she doesn't leave the office area immediately. I ask someone to call a security company and have guards start as soon as possible.

I drive home in a fog. I have no idea, no real idea that is, that my marriage is over. It hasn't hit me. When I get home, David is gone. Of course he is. Still, I don't really believe it.

Yep, it was a very, very bad week.

POST PETS.COM

What I didn't know was how bad it would get. I thought I'd mastered the art of the rebound. I mean, it's not exactly like I had a trauma-free childhood and yet, my nickname in school was Sunshine or Jewels. I always saw the glass as half-full. I could always find the humor.

I didn't realize that when you're older, life is different. You see the patterns in your past actions and they can actually trap you in the past because you assume that this is just how your life will always be. Sometimes, you create patterns when they aren't there, because you're miserable; you think you must have done something wrong, because you are in so much pain and time is running out and you can see very clearly that there won't be that many more do-overs in your future. If any.

And that's pretty much where I was — miserable, with no clear path out. Pets.com's very public failure combined with the dissolution of my marriage and entering mid-life left me in a place where all I saw were limitations and the things I didn't have. My career and my marriage were gone. My body was telling me it was becoming wrinkled and withered. My ovaries were not-so-politely informing me that I was a middle-aged woman and children were no longer an option. I was finished. I played this record over and over again and as I did, I kept falling farther away from myself, entering a dark cave of depression.

I became suspended in a strange, numbing nothing-ness. I didn't feel anything. And, just when I thought I'd never feel again, rage would surge through my body. I realized my numbness was masking anger. I could explode with little or no provocation. I was furious with the looks I saw in people's eyes when I confirmed I was the ex-CEO of Pets.com. I was angry at my ex-husband, angry at my dog that died of heart failure when I needed his little heart more than ever, angry at the happy women who had perfect marriages and great jobs and had never, ever, been publicly scrutinized. I felt hatred toward the women who knew their husbands would take care of them financially, not betray them financially. I wanted to be a woman with a tiny personality, feminine and smart and interesting with babies. Maybe only one baby. I was angry at everything I was and all that I would never be.

I saw myself as a different version of my mother — my body may not have betrayed me, but I betrayed myself and, like her, I was trapped. I was on my own slow deathwatch and I just didn't care one way or another. It went on and on and on.

And the worst part was that nothing was funny. My humor had been the only way I knew to heal and cope and like everything else, it had completely abandoned me.

Many Years Post Pets.com

As I write this, the date is July, 2008, more than seven years since I shut down Pets.com. I am flying back from a business trip in New York. I've been out meeting with the press talking about SmartNow.com. Oh man, oh man, am I getting Pets.com backwash thrown at me. Seven years after the fact and reporters keep asking me about my biggest mistakes; they want to discuss the Pets.com financial statements. One is particularly hostile to me. I feel battered and bruised. The entire Pets.com nightmare comes rushing back: My husband moving his things out of the house Thanksgiving weekend, 2000; reporters knocking on my door before eight in the morning in March, 2001 to ask me what I thought of the dotcom crash. Being at a dinner party and having a woman ask me if I am the same Julie Wainwright who ran Pets.com and then bursting out laughing saying, 'What were you thinking? Are you an idiot?' Me, excusing myself from the table to go to the bathroom to throw up and then promptly leaving the party, heading home that evening trying to talk myself back to near center thinking, 'Who in the hell is she? How rude is she?' yet still being stuck in my revolving emotions for days afterward. Wanting desperately to feel good again about something and not knowing how to take that first step.

But now is now, not all of those years ago and I need to focus. I have a television interview early tomorrow morning. I've been told by my public relations person, that the interviewer might be a little negative and will definitely ask me about Pets.com and what I did wrong. I'm just not that interested in rehashing the Pets.com financial losses. I decide instead to make a list of the biggest mistakes I made to clear my thoughts before I get on the air.

So, I start writing about my real mistakes. Not my business mistakes, but my LIFE mistakes. I finish writing them on the plane trip home and edit them before I leave for the interview. I post the article on SmartNow.com. I figure if anyone visits the site after the television interview, maybe, just maybe, someone will read this post. And maybe, it will help them if they are also struggling.

Here is what I wrote that day:

MISTAKE 1
I allowed others to define me.

As you saw, Pets.com received press worldwide when it launched and through out its short life. The company and I were covered on business sections of CNN, CNNfn, ABC, NBC, CBS, the BBC, Wall Street Journal, New York Times; I was in major magazines including Town and Country, and Shape. The Sock Puppet was in the Macy's Day Parade, on the red carpet at Oscar time and, as I recall, had a huge crush on Diane Sawyer. A crush she seemed to return, at least while they were on the air together.

As much press as Pets.com got when it looked like it would succeed — and believe me, it was up there with the most popular news items of the day — it got even more when it failed. I have a stack about 12 inches deep of press clippings, all about the failure of the company. The stack from the good times? It's about 3-inches deep.

The website chat rooms were equally balanced. There was one company that relished failure, called F*@%&Dcompany.com that was dedicated to the decline of companies. Disgruntled employees, and really anyone, vented anonymously about companies and people and spread all kinds of rumors. Pets.com got its share of community comments on this website. So did I, and they were not kind. During a job interview I actually had a venture capitalist hand me printouts of chatter from that site. He made me to read them in the conference room, then sat back and asked me to defend myself. I remember saying that it was a gossip site, whose main purpose was letting angry people vent anonymously and that I had no response to it. Later, the recruiter told me this individual circulated the same printouts during a closed-door session with other investors and they all decided I was not right for the job. When I heard that, I made up my mind to read everything bad ever written about me and Pets.com. I immersed myself in it. And pretty soon, I believed it.

Since the press and message boards declared me a complete failure, it must be true. And what happened next? I attracted new people and jobs that reinforced this.

HOW I MOVED ON

I got tired of living in the past. It's strangely comfortable to beat yourself up all the time, but it isn't nourishing. I took stock of myself and made the decision that I knew myself better than anyone else did. I am the only one who has taken my journey. I had failures and successes in the past. If I really looked at things truthfully, I had more successes than failures (although this may have been my biggest). I had acted honorably towards the Pets.com employees and the shareholders, but I hadn't treated myself with the same kindness.

I also came to recognize that most reactions to me were not personal. Almost none of the people writing about Pets had been an employee, knew an employee, run a company or even taken a risk. The anger that people threw in my direction was simply a reflection of their personal dreams being shattered. Maybe they needed a place to vent or some deeper demon was gripping them. Whatever it was, it was all about them; in fact, it had absolutely nothing to do with me. Even though Pets.com and its CEO were certainly an easy target.

Oddly enough, the venture capitalist that pulled out

the nasty comments was the trigger to my getting better. While that meeting was ghastly and it initially pushed me deeper into a bad space, it also forced me to deal with people's negativity. I realized that if I internalized this negative energy, it just whacked me in the gut and controlled me.

I actually began to view him as a teacher, and a test for me. Once I saw that his actions were a reflection of him and his disappointments, I could let go of my anger toward him. I applied the same principles to everyone I came across, even the people who posted on the snarky websites.

I also intrinsically knew that the minute I let anyone negative define my past, that past became my future by default. I had a choice: go along with someone else's perception of the world or get on with creating my own world. I didn't want to live my own version of the movie "Groundhog Day." I really wanted to heal my own wounds and start living again, so I made a conscious decision to separate my wounds from everyone else's. It's a funny thing too, because when I started to pay close attention to that tenet and I did so from a place of love, not fear, all that negativity lost its power. As far as I can tell, negativity needs energy, a reaction, to feed it.

MISTAKE 2
I built my image of myself on two main supporting pillars.

I defined myself in two distinct ways: a smart woman who could figure anything out; and a married woman, on the brink of entering middle age. I liked this picture of myself! If you had asked me then just how central they were to my core, I would have dismissed the notion with, "Oh, that's just a part of who I am!" But the truth is, when I stopped being both of things, my house of cards folded. Here is what I know now. I held tightly onto those two adjectives, smart and married, as a measurement of personal worth that left no room for me to just be a person, who accepted my own humanness. And when I couldn't use those adjectives to describe myself, I became in my mind, worthless. I never held anyone else to these standards, since I knew they were external measurements, but I didn't have the same compassion for myself.

You probably already figured out how the "smart" part was cultivated in my childhood. I had to figure out a lot of stuff all by myself. Couple that with my parent's dedication to making all of their children independent and self-sufficient and it becomes a fixed belief that doesn't allow mistakes. Whenever I asked my parents a question, their mantra was, "You are smart, what do you think?"

This worked out well for me as a child. I wasn't afraid of much. I loved solving problems. The idea of failure didn't even enter my consciousness. If another brain had learned something, then, I could too. I did recognize that some brains were significantly smarter than others, but that didn't diminish mine, it just showed me what was possible and inspired me. I made top honors in school. I never bought into being a "pretty" girl; I was the smart one.

And, then, boom! I was not smart enough for Pets. com. I fell flat on my face, publicly. After more than 20 years of pretty great business success, I was a flame-out. This utterly terrified me.

The second way I defined myself was as a married woman. I liked being married, belonging to a little tribe of two. What could be more wonderful than to be with someone you love; someone you are so comfortable with that you can strip away your outside defenses and just enjoy each other? What could be more terrible than being single and old? I'm not sure when I developed the premise that being married was integral to my self-worth. Certainly, there are societal pressures and perceptions of the value of being married that I unconsciously bought into, but it was deeper than that. I'm sure it stems from a need to feel safe and secure — something that was threatened in my childhood where death was regularly knocking.

Whatever the motivation, I identified strongly with the image of being married and couldn't imagine my life alone — even though I had been single for years prior to my marriage. In reality, I didn't have any security in my marriage; I was both sad and terribly lonely.

Within 48-hours both my marriage and my job were over. I felt my "support system" turn to dust. I crumbled.

HOW I MOVED ON

Where did this leave me? Lost. What did I do? I wallowed in a stew of distraction and depression for a while. Then, slowly, I started looking for something that would feed my soul.

I tried to get back to my essence, my best self. I love drawing and painting, so I started doing this again and working with art organizations. I love being around people who solve problems creatively, create art, think differently and express themselves uniquely. Watching and participating in the creative process started rejuvenating me.

I knew I had lost my sense of humor, which had always been a healing part of my life. So, I went in search of funny. I rented funny movies. I sought out laughter. I developed relationships with very loving people who laughed. I started to appreciate the absurdity of life again, especially my silly life.

I also got involved in my local community — not just by volunteering, but also by spending time with my neighbors and the locals. I developed a few routines, ensuring that I saw people who inspired me on a regular basis. This included spending time with a 70-something-year-old woman, Jeanie Brown, who owned the local coffee shop and vibrates with life. Jeanie, who is functionally illiterate, has a simple motto in life, "Don't look at what you can't do. Look at what you can do and make the most of it." And, slowly, I began to see myself as more than two key bullet points. I had always been well-rounded. I realized that all those who truly loved me didn't care if I was über successful, and they certainly did not want to see me in an unsatisfying marriage. Their love wasn't conditional. I learned that those pillars I'd propped myself up on all those years were just false security. I began to feel truly secure simply by being myself and really enjoying life.

Mistake 3
I stopped believing in myself.

You can see how the first and second mistakes lead to the third. For a long time, especially when it came to my own career, I operated from a place of fear. Fear of failure. Fear of rejection. And then, I failed. I wasn't so smart. In my mind, I was washed-up.

How I moved on

It dawned on me that by only seeing myself as a failure and nothing more, I was dying a very slow, painful death. That mental frame of reference sets up a whole series of bad events that continually reinforce each other. It's a vicious cycle. I saw my patterns of negative thinking influence actions and reactions by observing similar patterns in a dear friend. Sometimes your friends are wonderful mirrors.

Here is what my friend does. He believes he is really bad in relationships with women. Therefore, whenever he dates someone, the more he likes the person, the more he fears it will end badly. Because he fears it will end badly, he starts the cycle: he shouldn't contact the person because that person will find out how bad he is at relationships and reject him; he pulls away and then sure enough, the woman wants to know if there is something wrong. He hears this as, "What's wrong with you?" and he pulls back further and thinks, "wow, she knows I am damaged, guess I'm done here." At this point, he goes radio silent. The woman, of course gets angry with him for running hot and cold. He apologizes, acknowledging how terrible he is at relationships and with intimacy and, voila! He instantly becomes bad at both. The truth is, he is great friend who is easy to be around and with whom you can share all your secrets. He just doesn't perceive himself that way.

I was creating a similar dynamic in my life, especially as it applied to work. I believed that no one would hire me again and I would only be offered less desirable jobs. And, guess what? I was. And, I took them, thinking that was the best I could do. I chose to say yes to something inferior. I had to break this cycle and create a new vision for myself that was built on my strengths and passions.

I decided that if I believed in myself, I had to invest in myself. If I didn't invest in myself I couldn't expect others to do it, either.

I also needed to set goals again in life. Small ones and big ones. I figured if I accomplished the small ones, I'd reinforce that great feeling that comes with achievements. Once I reached the small ones, it wasn't a far reach for me to hit the bigger ones.

I made a vision board because I respond to visual cues. I pasted pictures and phrases that represented my goals - personal and professional - on white poster board. The most prominent goals were focused on me being successful in every part of my life, physical, emotional and spiritual. On the business side, I showed myself climbing the proverbial ladder and once again reaching for the stars. And when I had a good business plan in hand, I invested money in my own company. This is the first time I have started a company for myself.

MISTAKE 4
I stopped taking care of myself.

This goes hand-in-hand with investing in myself. I had gained weight over the years and stopped exercising. When Pets was collapsing, I started exercising again and the pounds had started to come off, so my physical health had started to improve. What I didn't realize is that my emotional health was deteriorating. I did not recognize my own depression. For at least two years after Pets shut down, I didn't care if I lived or died. I never actively tried to kill myself; that would go against my Mid-Western upbringing. I just didn't care.

I was also just starting to experience the first symptoms of peri-menopause, so I had to come terms with my own childlessness. I had curiously felt that if I was meant to have a child, then I would have gotten pregnant during my marriage. Not having children reinforced my indifference to life during this period. I didn't have children to take care of, so what was the point?

How I Moved On

In retrospect, I wish I had been more proactive with my mental health. I did not recognize my state of mind as depression. I mean, I wasn't crying every day, I didn't drive to the Golden Gate Bridge and contemplate jumping. But I was clearly depressed, and only years later did I realize how much I needed help. I should have seen a therapist and perhaps even gone on medication. I think it's important to point out that I did not fall into a depression. I slipped into one. I know some people who describe depression as something that descends on them rapidly and pulls them out of life's reach. That wasn't my experience. I had a great public face and a sad private one. I do think this is one of the dangers of living alone. It's virtually impossible to really see yourself — both the good and the bad — without the reflection in the eyes of those who truly love you. There isn't any perspective without that.

I pulled myself out of this by trying to really see beauty again (see Mistake Two, which also shows the healing power of art in my life). Once I started seeing beauty, I wanted to see more of it. Once I learned to let go of the anger and fear, I wanted to thrive.

I never stopped exercising during this period. I felt better after I worked out and let's face it, I liked being thinner. Exercise is critical to feeding the brain with oxygen and endorphins and I strongly believe exercising each day saved me from going deeper into depression. I know that sounds dramatic, but exercise does have a dramatic effect on your brain.

Special note: If you think you are depressed or know someone who is, then please get yourself or them help. Do not stay in that depressed place. Get help. If you do not have money to see a doctor, there are free clinics that will treat you. If you don't have a computer at home, your library does or a friend does. Please don't make excuses for not seeking help you can feel better. More information on depression is found in the last chapter of this book. I encourage you to read it.

Mistake 5:
Allowing my head to rule my heart.

If I had started with this one, it might have seemed trite. But it isn't. The head is the ego. Mine was shattered. And, yet, I kept relying on thinking and of course, rationalizing. I didn't realize that I couldn't think my way to a better place. I didn't trust my heart energy. I didn't acknowledge that there was a deeper flow to life and that I would be supported if I went with it.

How I moved on

To be honest, I'm not sure I have moved past this, but I am doing better. It's a work in progress. During my darkest periods, I would logic myself out of them. Convincing myself I had to do something, sometimes as simple as getting out of bed and exercising, had a place in moving beyond my depression. Pure thinking and determination alone would not have opened my life up again and set me on the right course. Doing things that filled my heart with love and learning to trust myself enough to follow my heart...those were the key. That meant

I had to sit still, listen quietly and do regular gut checks. And then, like everything else, I needed positive reinforcement I was on the right track.

Small successes showed me I was safe and slowly I began to let my heart make some decisions. These decisions resulted in tremendous support, love and kindness. I had to learn to let go of fear. It meant learning to trust myself, my spirit and something greater than me, which connects us all.

POSTSCRIPT:
BLESSINGS, MIRACLES AND SEXY MOMENTS

As a child, I used to pray to God to make me wise. When I think of that little girl on her knees every night praying for wisdom, I have two strong reactions. Mostly, I just want to cradle her because I deeply love her and her soulful intent. Another part of me wants to reach back in time and shout at her, "Be careful what you ask for!"

I can now say my childhood prayer was answered and continues to be answered daily and I am so thankful.

The days and years that followed Pets.com were some of the most transformative of my life. I desperately sought normal. I never achieved that. I landed someplace richer and stronger. I feel like my growth grew beyond what I imagined and I feel so blessed. That doesn't mean every day is goodness and light; of course not! Life didn't change. As the saying goes, I did. There is an expression that goes, "When you change the way you look at things, the things you look at change." I have seriously challenging moments when fear takes hold of me. But I don't stay there and I have been able to love more deeply than I ever thought possible.

Here's what else happened: As I got more authentic, I really started embracing being a woman again. On the road to being a Working Woman, I made significant efforts to de-sexualize myself in the workplace, which, by the way, is not a bad thing as long as you leave it in the office. The problem was, I had forgotten how to turn it on when I wasn't working. Being in a bad marriage didn't help that situation. The first time a man flirted with me, I didn't know what to do with the vibe he was putting out. I blushed, stuttered and walked away from him.

I'm still awkward with a flirt that comes my way. But at least I know it when I see it now. I gave myself permission to be more real with my femininity and embrace it totally. It's fun re-integrating being a woman back into my person.

Also, writing about my mistakes has brought amazing

people into my life and created some interesting interviews. BBC Radio 4 interviewed me because the DJ stumbled upon the blog and felt it resonated with him and would do so with his listeners. Popular U.S. radio host, Doug Stephan, interviewed me for the same reason. As did Joanie Greggains, another talk show host in the Bay Area. Joanie and Doug have become my friends and life is richer for them. I've also had strangers come up to me and thank me for writing the blog. Their actions have touched me deeply.

ON DEPRESSION

I asked Angela Mohan, a Licensed Marriage and Family Therapist who has extensive experience in treating depression, to write about it. She gives you practical definitions of depression along with specific actions you can do to move past this debilitating disease. The following is from her.

"The blues", "down in the dumps", "feeling low." We've all been there before. That horrible draining feeling of discouragement, of bleakness, of sighing and wondering when it will all get better. It's a feeling that has probably visited most of us at some point in our lives. Sometimes we can pretty easily identify the causes of those feelings; our hormones, stress, fatigue, work, our husband/partners/friends, the holidays. But sometimes the causes elude us. And how can we tell if it is something more, something other than a passing mood or stressful time that will resolve itself on its own? How do we know if we ourselves (or someone we love) has been hit with a depression that is more than just a passing feeling?

One of the ways to think about depression is on a continuum. On the one side is a somewhat passing feeling that stays for a few hours or even for a day or two, and that works itself out and gets us back into balance without too much being lost along the way. Further along the continuum are feelings of sadness that don't go away readily, perhaps bouts of crying or constant irritability, difficulty getting up in the morning and a more general sense of malaise that is still manageable, though with perhaps more effort needed on our parts to address it.

At the far end of the continuum is where you want to feel better but you just can't seem to muster the energy or the ability to make yourself feel better. When you want to take care of yourself but all you do is reach for the remote at the end of the day and spend every night burrowing deeper under the covers and wondering if it will ever get better. This is the place where you need to ask yourself if this is a "passing thing" or something more serious.

There are times in all of our lives when things are difficult and demanding and stressful. Sometimes, (most times) we are able to roll with the punches and get back on our feet without too much trouble. But sometimes we get hit and we stay down. We need to know the difference between a "passing" feeling and a depression that won't budge.

There are a number of symptoms that characterize clinical depression and it's important to be able to identify them so that we know how best to help ourselves and to mobilize our resources. But know that you don't have to have all of the following symptoms in order to be considered depressed. Sometimes you might just have a few of the symptoms, but they are so relentless that they interfere with your daily functioning. Depression is pervasive and severe, and all of these manifestations need to be taken seriously. Only you know what is or is not "usual" for you. And be sure not to discount your feelings or these symptoms; often depressed people (women especially) wait to get help because they minimize their pain, thinking, "Well, my life isn't so bad. Lots of people have things worse than I do. What's wrong with me? I just have to stop complaining."

Some of the symptoms/manifestations to be aware of include:

- Your energy is shot

- You have difficulty sleeping and either sleep way too little or way too much

- You have stopped returning phone calls and e-mails, and you don't want to go out socially anymore, even though you usually enjoy going out

- You have difficulty concentrating or getting the simplest things done

- You have difficulty making decisions even though decision-making hasn't posed a problem for you in the past

- You're irritable. Not the usual "sometimes life and people can be annoying" irritable, but the "everything and everyone pisses me off" irritable

- Your eating is off (too much or too little) and you lose weight or gain weight

- The things that you used to enjoy now leave you feeling empty, and you begin to hear yourself saying things like, "What's the use? Nothing matters anyway."

- You feel depressed or other people who know and love you begin to say that they think you are depressed. (sometimes we don't recognize it from the inside out)

- You have feelings of worthlessness, inappropriate guilt, feelings of overwhelming hopelessness, helplessness, and a pessimistic view on things

- Your self esteem plummets

- You have physical symptoms/aches and pains including, (but not necessarily limited to) headaches, back pains, gastrointestinal issues, muscle aches and pains

- You have recurring thoughts of death or thoughts of suicide

- You have made suicide attempts or made a plan to commit suicide

- Your depression is not due to a medical condition (talk

to your doctor!) or to the physiological effects of sub-stances (prescription or non-prescription)

What might have started as a passing mood has now turned into a biologically and psychologically based depression. This isn't just "the blues" anymore. This won't go away on its own. This is when you need to get your little self some support because one of the most pernicious aspects of depression when it reaches this level is the sense/fear that it won't get better. (And this is also the time to say something to that friend you are worried about. I know it can be difficult, but ladies, we've got to look out for one another, and if your friend is drowning in one of these depressions, believe me, she needs you to say something and to reach out your hand to her)

There are many reasons and/or causes that women get depressed. Among them are traumatic life experiences, the death of a loved one, family stresses, job pressures, the birth of a baby bringing with it post-partum depression, substance use or chemical dependency (either prescribed or non), and existential crisis questions like, "what is the meaning of it all? Do I matter?" There are also hormonal fluctuations that may impact a woman's chemistry and result in a depression.

But at the heart of depression and its management is the fact that regardless of the reason, clinical depression is debilitating and pervasive. It can cause significant impairment at work, at home, in your personal relationships, in your sense of well-being in the world. It MUST be actively managed, regardless of its origin. Depression, unlike sadness or grief, won't "go away on its own" given the passage of time. In fact, because of the downward spiraling nature of an entrenched depression, if nothing is done to reverse the damaging effects and manifestations, it will very likely get much worse. So, even if you don't feel like it, (and you won't) you have to start finding ways to manage your depression.

So, how do you manage your depression once you've identified it? Well, you can certainly try psychotropic medications (anti-depressants) but some people don't want to take that route. It's important that you get as much information as you can regarding psychotropic medication in order for you to evaluate whether or not it is the right depression management choice for you. Ask your doctor to discuss the pros and cons with you to help you make the best decision for yourself. And remember, psychotropic medications are there to help give you the initial "helping hand" to get you back on track until your other internal resources kick in. Most people tend to be on psychotropic meds for only the amount of time that it takes them to initiate and solidify other coping strategies. Beginning meds doesn't mean you'll be on them for the rest of your life. They may be just what you need though to get you out of the darkest part of the depression until you feel well enough to exchange the meds for other self-management skills.

Ah yes, and speaking of feeling better, it can be really tempting to turn to other things to make you feel better, like alcohol and mood-altering substances. (Prescription or non-prescription) But, they will only make you feel better temporarily and are likely to cause an even greater downward spiral once the effects have worn off. So, as tempting as it may be to "self medicate", don't. I promise you it won't take you where you want to be, which is free from the debilitating effects of this depression.

If you don't like the idea of psychotropic meds, you can try talk therapy which will help you feel supported and provide you with some tools to start feeling better. Talk therapy may help you bring to light some of the ways your depression is manifesting itself as well as highlight any underlying issues that might be exacerbating your depression. There has been a great deal of research done regarding the connection between depression and "negative self talk" which are the negative ways we talk to ourselves about the things that are happening to us in our lives, or about how we feel and think about ourselves. I know you are all familiar with the voice in your head that is relentlessly critical of you, or is the voice of discouragement, or whispers to you that "you just can't do it." Talk therapy might assist you in identifying those voices and dealing more effectively with them. It also might help you in identifying any long-term issues that you've been carrying around with you and that have gone unresolved all these years. Oftentimes resolution of these issues can help alleviate some of the symptoms of depression.

If you are not interested in talk therapy, then perhaps a visit to your local bookstore is in order. There's the seminal book by Dr. David Burns called Feeling Good, which will give you some user-friendly depression-busting exercises. It is the perfect book if you want to learn mood management strategies that will last you a lifetime. It's written for "regular" people so it is not filled with incomprehensible psychobabble or tricky techniques that you can't make head or tails of. There's also a Feeling Good Handbook that can be useful. If not this book, then check out any of the books on depression in the self-help section, and find one that works for you. Trust yourself. You'll know when a particular title "speaks" to you. Baring a bookstore visit, try the Internet. You'll find endless articles and resources that might point you in a direction that might help you.

Certainly healthy nutrition and regular exercise help, although don't change/add anything without your doctors' ok. The "feel-good chemical" endorphins that get released as a result of exercise can help you feel better and the healing benefits of exercise have been proven in study after study. Of course, one of the most common symptoms of depression though is a lack of energy and/or a lack of motivation, which can make exercise seem like an impossible task.

Other things to add to your depression-busting arsenal are yoga, journaling, meditation, long, hot soaks in your bathtub, lunches with a friend, hobbies, volunteer activities, reconnecting at your place of worship, playing with your dog.

In short, any activity that will help you feel better. But again, know that you might not feel like doing any of these; that is in the very nature of some of the symptoms of depression. Try not to beat yourself up over this. As wise Eleanor Roosevelt said, "Do what you can, with what you have, where you are."

No matter what route you decide to take to manage your depression, get some support during your journey. Let your friends and loved ones know you're struggling; give them a chance to be there for you. This is not one of those things you want to do on your own. Reach out. Hang in there. It will get better.

About Angela Mohan: Angela Mohan, M.F.T., has been a licensed marriage and family therapist for the past 15 years. She has built successful private practices in Los Angeles and Ventura counties, and teaches law and ethics at Pacifica Graduate Institute. Ms. Mohan, often described as a "fun," "enthusiastic," and "lively" speaker, offers seminars at USC, UCLA, Cal State-Los Angeles and Cal State-Long Beach. Ms. Mohan is a published author and professional speaker and has served on the Board of Directors for the California Association of Marriage and Family Therapists. She is also a Certified Gottman Method Couples' Therapist and works extensively with teens. Ms. Mohan can be reached at angelamohan@sbcglobal.net.

PLEASE NOTE: This information is designed for education purposes only. You should not rely on this information as a substitute for, nor do this replace, professional medical advice, diagnosis or treatment. If you have any concerns or questions about your health, you should always consult a physician or another health-care professional including psychiatrist or psychologist. Do not disregard, avoid or delay obtaining medical or health related advice from you're your health-care professional.

And, with that, I'm ending this little book of big mistakes.

ABOUT THE AUTHOR, JULIE WAINWRIGHT

Julie started her career at The Clorox Company in brand management. She leaped into the world of personal computer software in her 20s after seeing Visacalc do P&L calculations in seconds versus her hand-cranked "what if" scenarios that took hours each day. By the age of 30, she was a group product manager for a $125 Million business. She was promoted to CEO after she successfully turned around Berkeley Systems with the introduction of the popular game "You Don't Know Jack". After the sale of Berkeley Systems, Julie joined Reel.com as CEO. That company was sold for nearly $100 Million dollars. She then became CEO of Pets.com — the first site for pets ever funded. Eight others (that she knows about) were funded after it. Pets.com pulled its Sock out of the pack, created an enduring brand and achieved over revenue of $46 Million in just nine months in 2000. She closed the company to return money to shareholders the same day her husband told her he wanted divorce. The combination of the two resulted in a spiritual journey.

She is the founder of SmartNow.com, which is dedicated to giving women the best health, nutrition and fitness information.

She has appeared on all major networks including ABC, NBC, CBS, and the BBC. She has been featured in many magazines from those with a business slant to lifestyle magazines such as InShape and Town and Country. She was honored to speak at the 2000 California Governor's Conference on Women and Family. She has spoken at Harvard and Purdue universities and has sat on many business boards including: Wizards of the Coast and Baker and Taylor; and not-for-profit boards including the San Francisco Art Institute, Magic Theatre and Headlands Center for the Arts.

ReBoot is her first book.

You can email Julie at: Julie@Smartnow.com.

ACKNOWLEDGEMENTS

There are several people who were instrumental in me writing this book. The list is long, almost as long as the dedication! Here we go:

First, a big thank you to Royana Black, my editor, who provided keen insight and guidance.

And, to Ken Monnens, a man of rare intelligence, energy, creativity and generosity, thank you for always saying yes, even when you are tired and pulled in so many directions.

Thank you to Joanie Greggains who kept pushing me to write the book. Your energy and kindness could light the planet.

Thank you to the mystery man, you are a loving teacher.

Catherine Moy, I know I doubted you when you told me I could write this book. Thank you for your encouragement.

Thank you, Holly Root! Here's to a long and prosperous relationship.

And, lastly thank you to Angela Mohan, whose life is dedicated to helping others be the best they can.

2273956

ISBN: 978-1-0878-5437-3 (RETAIL STORES)

ISBN: 978-1-73229528-5 (KDP AMAZON PAPERBACK)

ISBN: 978-1-73229527-8 (BARNES AND NOBLE HAARDBACK)

ISBN: 978-1-66358807-4 (BARNES AND NOBLE PAPERBACK)

Library of Congress Control Number: 2020919846

Publishing Services by Stanton Publishing House

FOREWORD

The President We Need

As National Director of Priests for Life, I have worked in the national political arena since 1994, helping pro-life candidates to get elected, providing input to campaigns about Catholic and pro-life issues, strategizing and praying with pro-life lawmakers, and working with the Republican National Committee to keep the abortion issue high on the priority list, as it already is with a significant portion of the American electorate.

Never have I been so encouraged in this work as I have been by President Donald Trump. Growing up just outside of New York City, I have observed him much of my life. I have been privileged to serve both of his presidential campaigns on his Catholic advisory boards and as National Co-Chair of Pro-life Voices for Trump.

From the beginning, through my encounters with him and with his close advisors, I was told that if he were elected, he would do what all other pro-life presidents have done "and more." Those words have come true practically every day since.

This is a man who sizes up problems with a positive, "can-do" spirit, receives advice not just from experts but from anyone whose ideas make sense, commits himself to a plan and does not back away from his critics. Not only does he keep his promises, but he keeps more promises than he makes!

He is a man who believes in the power of prayer. On election night, when it was clear that he was going to win, he was on the phone with one of the pastors who advises him, and declared to the pastor, "It was the prayers!" Asked by another pastor how he wanted to be remembered, the President responded, "I want to be remembered as the President who prayed more than any other."

I have observed his prayerfulness and his pro-life commitment up close. And it is no exaggeration to say that in my ministry as a priest and a pro-life leader, I have received more encouragement and strength in my mission from President Donald Trump than from the leaders of my own Church.

This is a man who knows how to connect with the pro-life community, with the Faith community, and with the American people. You feel that connection, whether you're listening to him address the nation or engage in a private conversation. It's the reason he drew to the polls so many who had never voted before; it's the reason why his political rallies have been met not only with cheers of "Four More Years," but with the unprecedented and now regular chant, "We love you!"

Why Trump?

Memories of A Journey of Faith
Hope and Love

Alveda C. King (signature)

Evangelist Alveda C. King

FOREWORD BY REV. FRANK PAVONE

"You are the elite," he declares. "We – not I – but we will keep on winning," he tells the people. His campaign, as he points out, is not just a campaign but a movement. He reminds us that the attacks on him are attacks on all of us, and all we hold dear. "I am fighting for you," he declares, and that's why the crowds respond, "We love you!"

Being blessed to have on our fulltime Priests for Life pastoral team Evangelist Alveda King, whom I've known since 1999, she and I have had memorable moments together in the presence of the President. Each time, it was clear that he listened, understood, spoke our language and fought for our cause.

In the pro-life community, a pivotal moment we always recall was in the third debate with Hillary Clinton. On the question of abortion, he took what I have always considered the best possible approach with the Democrats: expose their extremism. He said to her,

"In the ninth month, you can take the baby and rip the baby out of the womb of the mother just prior to the birth of the baby. Now you can say that that's OK and Hillary can say that that's OK, but it's not OK with me… That's not acceptable."

As Ralph Reed recounts in his book For God and Country, Kellyanne Conway remarked that although the campaign had prepared for the abortion question in debate prep, Donald Trump's response had not been part of those preparations. Said Kellyanne, "That came directly from his heart."

We learned a similar thing from Mick Mulvaney who, when recounting the preparation for the President's 2019 State of the Union Address, told the National Catholic Prayer Breakfast that as the President was reviewing the draft of the speech, which contained a section about abortion, he took pen to paper and, entirely on his own initiative, he added more words to that pro-life section.

Both Alveda and I have seen firsthand the faith, the generosity of spirit, the humility, and the kindness of heart of Donald J. Trump. And we have seen the fruits of those virtues in the beautiful family he has raised. Our interactions with his children at various times have shown us the tremendous respect and love they have for their father, as well as the integrity he has inspired in them. "By their fruits you will know them," the Lord told us.

We have also seen how he inspires those who have worked for him, whether in the Campaign or in the White House, or in his previous business life. Every one of these individuals that I have met and spoken with have the highest regard for him, and have found in him the encouragement to pursue their own vocations with renewed energy, determination, and positive spirit.

Why Trump?

As President, Donald J. Trump unites our nation. His critics are not only consistently wrong about him, but they are wrong by astronomical measures. Far from being divisive, he is the one who rallies America because of success. He believes success is a unifying force, and he proves it.

He points out that prior to the pandemic, he was having more and more people from across the political and ideological spectrum come to him in a cooperative spirit. Why? Because they saw an economy stronger than any we had ever experienced. They saw successes on the international level that previous administrations considered impossible to achieve. They, along with more and more of the American people, were convinced the country was moving in the right direction.

Success unites.

And the principles of America unite. These principles, of God-given rights - starting with the right to life - of equality and freedom, of faith and family, are principles that President Trump articulates constantly and implements in his Administration's policies. He does what he is empowered to do to weaken the abortion industry, and calls on Congress to protect children in the womb and to end infanticide. He removes government regulations so that businesses can have the breathing space to grow and thrive. He protects free speech on campuses and in the pulpit, and the choice of parents to send their children to the schools of their choice.

He values our history and makes sure our children learn it accurately. He knows we must unite around our national symbols by loving our flag, respecting our anthem, and proudly reciting our pledge, including the words "under God." As he says in his rally speeches, "We are one movement, we are one people, one family, and one glorious nation under God."

That is a unifier. That is the kind of President we need. And that is the President Alveda and I have come to know, to love, and to proudly support.

Fr. Frank Pavone, National Director, Priests for Life

FR. FRANK PAVONE is one of the most prominent pro-life leaders in the world. Originally from New York, he was ordained in 1988 by Cardinal John O'Connor, and since 1993 has served full-time in pro-life leadership with his bishop's permission. He is the National Director of Priests for Life, the largest pro-life ministry in the Catholic Church. He is also the President of the National Pro-life Religious Council, and the National Pastoral Director of the Silent No More Awareness Campaign and of Rachel's Vineyard, the world's largest ministry of healing after abortion. He travels throughout the country, to an average of four states every week, preaching and teaching against abortion. He produces programs regularly for religious and secular radio and television networks. He was asked by Mother Teresa to speak in India on the life issues, and has addressed the pro-life caucus of the United States House of Representatives. The Vatican appointed him to the Pontifical Academy for Life and to the Pontifical Council for the Family, which coordinates the pro-life activities of the Catholic Church. He was present at the bedside of Terri Schiavo as she was dying and was an outspoken advocate for her life. He was invited by members of the Class of 2009 at Notre Dame to lead an alternate commencement ceremony for those students who refused to attend the ceremony in which President Obama was honored. Fr. Frank was invited by members of Congress to preach at the prayer service they had in the Capitol just prior to the vote on health care reform. He received the "Proudly Pro-life Award" by the National Right to Life Committee, and numerous other pro-life awards and honorary doctorates. He is the author of four books, Ending Abortion, Not Just Fighting It; Pro-life Reflections for Every Day; Abolishing Abortion, and Proclaiming the Message of Life. Norma McCorvey, the "Jane Roe" of the Supreme Court's Roe vs. Wade abortion decision, called Fr. Frank "the catalyst that brought me into the Catholic Church."

PREFACE

Connecting the dots during the course of a season of transformation in America: My response to inquiries as to why I support, pray for, and vote for President Donald J. Trump.

Donald J. Trump is my President. I've got my vote, and my prayers. Both are in favor of President Trump and his 'promises made and promises kept.' These advances have not only blessed the Black communities of America; all Americans, born and unborn, are included. That's my short answer as to "Why Trump?"

When I first considered writing a book about President 45, I was intrigued by his twitter fame. I toyed with titles such as "The Real Donald Trump," and "@therealdonaldjtrump." Over the last almost five years now, if you consider the time with the campaign and the Trump Administration, so many people have asked me why I support this president. Never mind that I have supported many presidents in my lifetime of seventy years; with countless visits to the White House over the years. Until now, I have never had so much interest in my presidential choices. People either love me or hate me for my support of President 45. There is no middle road this time; no in-between. Here in 2020 the highly contested U.S. Presidential Election looming, the public climate is so polarizing that one must deal with either Trumpmania

Why Trump?

or Trump Derangement Syndrome. There doesn't seem to be an in-between anymore.

Prior to writing this book I never really sat down and formally researched the life of "The Real Donald J. Trump." Once I began to examine the life and times of our President for the purpose of writing a journal account of what for me has become an unlikely and totally unexpected "friendship" with President Trump and his family, I began to realize that the old saying that "nothing in life is ever really an accident" is true. I also realized while compiling these chronicles, that America had come to another transformational season and that my journey was not only coinciding with the trajectory of our President, I realized that the whole world was about to be turned upside, again.

As I began to journal the steps that led me to becoming a "spiritual advisor" in the "Trump Diversity Coalition Machine," I began to realize that there were certain series of events in this journey that were not serendipitous in nature.

Actually, early in the process of researching for this book, and studying the life of President Trump, a cursory online exploration of President Trump's life opened up a new viewpoint for me. His history led me to realize that there are contrasts and comparisons in our seemingly polar opposite lifestyles that would one day turn out to be a perfectly asymmetrical explanation as to why circumstances that led to my writing this book were meant to be.

Okay, I know that asymmetrical means that something or someone is imperfectly fit or knit to something or someone. However, as human events go, harmony can be found in the most uncommon and imperfect situations. This is the basis of this book, based upon comparisons, differences and coinciding paths and trajectories that have led to a 21st century convergence of ideologies and strategies in the lives of two unlikely American dream keepers, Donald J. Trump and Alveda Celeste King.

Much of this journaled history about both of us can be found as public record, primarily in Wikipedia. I make this true confession regarding the use of the online research with this caveat: Wiki is not an encyclopedia. It is a tool all too commonly used as a shortcut and substitute for deeper research. As a college professor of nineteen years, I often reminded my students that shortcuts of opinion masquerading as research should always be backed up with viable and provable facts.

Having said this, prayerfully, having completed the pages herein, readers will discover enough of interest to cause everyone to want to dig deeper into those points of interest that stand out for them. For now, in order to begin to make some sense of this journey, let's just start with a look at the life of Donald J. Trump. After that, we'll take a look at some of Alveda's experiences on planet earth.

Donald John Trump was born on June 14, 1946, at the Jamaica Hospital in the borough of Queens, New York City. His father was Frederick Christ Trump, a Bronx-born real estate developer, whose own parents were German immigrants. His mother was Scottish-born housewife and socialite Mary Anne MacLeod Trump. Trump grew up in the Jamaica Estates neighborhood of Queens, and attended the Kew-Forest School from kindergarten through seventh grade.

At age thirteen, he was enrolled in the New York Military Academy, a private boarding school. He excelled at sports. His favorite sport was golf, and he was a tight end on the football team in his freshman and sophomore years. In 1964, Trump enrolled at Fordham University.

Two years later he transferred to the Wharton School of the University of Pennsylvania after an interview with an admissions officer who had been a classmate of Trump's brother Fred. While at Wharton, he worked at the family business, Elizabeth Trump & Son, graduating in May 1968 with a B.S. in economics.

Why Trump?

Donald J. Trump received his degree from the Wharton School at the University of Pennsylvania. He took charge of his family's real estate business in 1971, renamed it The Trump Organization, and expanded it from Queens and Brooklyn into Manhattan. The company built or renovated skyscrapers, hotels, casinos, and golf courses. Trump later started various side ventures, mostly by licensing his name. He managed the company until his 2017 inauguration. He co-authored several books, including The Art of the Deal. He owned the Miss Universe and Miss USA beauty pageants from 1996 to 2015, and produced and hosted The Apprentice, a reality television show, from 2003 to 2015.

Religion

President Trump is a Presbyterian. His ancestors were Lutheran on his paternal grandfather's side in Germany and Presbyterian on his mother's side in Scotland. His parents married in a Presbyterian church in 1936. As a child, he attended the First Presbyterian Church in Jamaica, Queens, where he had his confirmation. In the 1970s, his parents joined the Marble Collegiate Church in Manhattan, part of the Reformed Church. The pastor at Marble, Norman Vincent Peale, ministered to Trump's family and mentored him until Peale's death in 1993.

Why Trump?

Trump Family in 1960's

(The next section, sourced from Wikipedia, is written in third person, to maintain continuity of flow.)

Alveda Celeste King (born January 22, 1951) is an American activist, author, and former state representative for the 28th District in the Georgia House of Representatives.

She is a niece of civil rights leader Martin Luther King Jr. and daughter of civil rights activist the Rev. A. D. King and his wife, Naomi Barber King. She is a Fox News Channel contributor. She once served as a senior fellow at the Alexis de Tocqueville Institution, a conservative Washington, D.C. think tank. She is a former member of the Georgia House of Representatives and the founder of Alveda King Ministries.

Why Trump?

Childhood and family

Alveda King was born in Atlanta, Georgia. She was the first of five children of A. D. King, the younger brother of Martin Luther King Jr., and his wife Naomi (Barber) King. King says her mother wanted to abort her, so she could continue college, but her grandfather was able to persuade her to keep her child. When she was 12, her father became a leader of the Birmingham campaign while serving as pastor at the First Baptist Church of Ensley in Birmingham, Alabama. Later that same year, King's house was bombed by opponents to the civil rights movement.

In 1969 her father, A. D. King, was found dead in the pool at his home. The cause of death was listed as an accidental drowning.

Martin Luther King Sr. wrote in his autobiography, "Alveda had been up the night before, she said, talking with her father and watching a television movie with him. He'd seemed unusually quiet . . . and not very interested in the film. But he had wanted to stay up and Alveda left him sitting in an easy chair, staring at the TV, when she went off to bed. I had questions about A. D.'s death, and I still have them now. He was a good swimmer. Why did he drown? I don't know—I don't know that we will ever know what happened."

Why Trump?

Education

King studied journalism and sociology as an undergraduate, and she received a Master of Arts degree in business management from Central Michigan University. She received an honorary doctorate from Saint Anselm College.

Public office

From 1979 until 1983, King represented the 28th District in the Georgia House of Representatives. The district included Fulton County, and King served as a Democrat.

In 1983, King became a "born again Christian." Following in the footsteps of her grandfather, Alveda "gave up drinking hard liquor. Granddaddy's father and my daddy had a problem with alcohol; so, granddaddy didn't partake. It made sense to me to do the same."

As an elected official, State Representative of Georgia District 28, King is noted for her sponsorship of legislation such as turning right on red lights; warning of fetal alcohol syndrome, court ordered counseling for victims of domestic violence and the MLK Holiday bill.

In 1984 King ran for the seat of Georgia's 5th congressional district in the U.S. House of Representatives. King challenged incumbent Representative Wyche Fowler. Fowler's predecessor, Andrew Young, endorsed Hosea Williams, who also challenged Fowler in the primary; Williams was one of Martin Luther King Jr.'s most trusted lieutenants and perhaps best known for organizing and leading the first Selma March.

Coretta Scott King did not endorse her niece. Young, who had given up the seat to serve as U.S. ambassador to the UN, and Williams approached King and asked her to end her campaign for the seat so that she could dedicate more time to her family. Young later apologized for what he called "some blatantly chauvinistic remarks." She did not withdraw. With the black vote split, Fowler defeated both King and Williams in the primary. That was the last time she ran for elective office. However, since then, she has publicly stated that she is a "Frederick Douglass Republican."

King is a member of the Frederick Douglass Bicentennial Commission, having been nominated to the position by President Donald Trump in 2018.

Presidential politics

In 1984, as a Democrat, King supported the Reverend Jesse Jackson for president. In the late 1990's, lured by the platforms for school choice and the fight to keep the "ten commandments" in the public square, King first became an "Independent." At the end of the twentieth century, King made a public announced that she had become a Republican. Taken under the wings of The Republican Vanguard and other African American conservatives, King became a presidential appointee in the administration of George W. Bush.

In 2008, King endorsed then candidate Sam Brownback for president. When Brownback stepped out of the race prior to the primaries, King was looking towards Mike Huckabee as her next favorite. However, having experienced a "spiritual awakening in 1983 when she became a "born again Christian," King had another epiphany. She was leaning towards "accepting a call" to become a Christian Evangelist, and was convinced that God wanted her to stop endorsing political candidates and to start praying for them.

From that time forward, King began accepting the moniker of "spiritual advisor." In that new role, she attends and speaks at prayer meetings, and on "prayer calls."

Later, in 2012, as a "prayer advisor," King supported Herman Cain for president and defended him from sexual harassment claims, saying, "A woman knows a skirt-chaser" and "Herman Cain is no skirt-chaser." She co-founded Women for Cain.

In 2016, King joined Donald Trump in the 2016 presidential election, stating, "I pray that all polar opposites learn to Agape Love, live, and work together as brothers and sisters—or perish as fools. While I voted for Mr. Trump, my confidence remains in God, for life, liberty, and the pursuit of happiness. Prayers for president-elect Trump, Congressman Lewis, and everyone including leaders."

Views and activism

Pro-life activism

King is the Executive Director of Civils Rights for The Unborn with Priests for Life. She is a dedicated pro-life activist. She had two abortions before adopting pro-life views following the birth of one of her children and her becoming a born-again Christian in 1983. King frames the issue as one of racial discrimination; she has referred to abortion as "womb-lynching" and accused Planned Parenthood of profiting from "aborting black babies." In 1996 she denounced her aunt Coretta Scott King's support for abortion rights. Angela D. Dillard classifies King as among most prominent black figures in the American religious right.

In 1994, according to Fox News, Alveda King has "long argued" that Dr. King was a Republican; she later wrote that she regretted the statement, writing "I said that without having all the facts" and noting that according to his own memoirs, King in fact was neither a Democrat or a Republican.

After civil rights leader Rosa Parks died in 2005, Alveda King called Parks an inspiration for the pro-life cause, likening the injustice of racial segregation to abortion.

2010 "Restoring Honor" Rally

King spoke at Glenn Beck's "Restoring Honor" rally at the Lincoln Memorial in August 2010. ABC News reported that in King's speech, she hoped that "white privilege will become human privilege and that America will soon repent of the sin of racism and return itself to honor."

Support of Natural Heterosexual Marriage

King has spoken out against same-sex marriage. In 2010 she equated same-sex marriage to genocide at a rally in Atlanta, saying, "We don't want genocide. While we love everyone, we don't want to diminish the human race or destroy the sacred institution of marriage." In a 2015 essay, she wrote that "life is a human and civil right, so is procreative marriage. We must now go back to the beginning, starting with Genesis, and teach about God's plan for marriage."

Personal life

King has been married and divorced three times. Her first marriage was to Jerry Ellis. Her second husband was Eddie Clifford Beal. Her third was to Israel Tookes. She is the mother of "six living children, two aborted, and one miscarriage."

Works

King has written the following books:

For generations to come: Poetry by Alveda King Beal (as Alveda King Beal) (1986)

The Arab Heart (as Alveda King Beal) (1986)

I Don't Want Your Man, I Want My Own (2001)

Sons of Thunder: The King Family Legacy (2003)

Who We Are In Christ Jesus (2008)

How Can the Dream Survive If We Murder the Children? Abortion is Not a Civil Right! (2008)

King Rules: Ten Truths for You, Your Family, and Our Nation to Prosper (2014)

America Return To God (2017)

GG's Home for the Holidays Cookbook (2017)

King Truths: 21 Keys to Unlocking Your Spiritual Potential (2018)

Slavery, Racism, Abortion and the Female Psyche: A Spiritual Perspective (2018)

A Pictorial History of the National Black Pro-Life Movement (2019)

The Spirit of the Dream (2019)

We're Not Colorblind (2020)

King, a self-proclaimed "Renaissance Woman," has produced the following musical works:

She released the CD, Let Freedom Ring in 2005, and Tender Moments Alone with God in 2018. She has appeared in film and television as both Alveda King and Alveda King Beal. The Human Experience, a 2010 documentary film, featured commentary from King.

She has produced or co-produced many documentaries and music videos, including the video "Latter Rain" (2005; and co-executive produced Pray for America. She's also Executive Producer of the movie Roe vs Wade.

Young A. D. King and Family in 1956

Why Trump?

Again, these cursory yet detailed online bios of President Trump and Alveda King may cause the reader to desire to know more about the persons who are the topic of this journal. Even as I read about President Trump's life and even some details about my own experiences, I find that I have forgotten many of the trails I've traveled. While reading President Trump's bio, I must admit that prior to 2015, I've never really known him, although I've admired him from afar for many years.

One thing I've discovered while writing this book is that we have very little, yet very much in common. In other words, when peripherals collide, convergence is imminent. The ancillary concept is often closely affiliated with the primary issue at hand... The answer of the question? Why Trump? in context to the support of Alveda King for America's President will be unraveled in the pages ahead.

Comparisons:

Donald J. Trump	Alveda Celeste King
President of the United States	Christian Evangelist
Caucasian Male	African American Female
Billionaire	Middle Class
Born into Wealth	Born into Christian Ministry
Successful Businessman, Humanitarian	Civil Rights Activist, Evangelist
Golfer	Arts Lover
Fast Food Lover	Organic Foods Enthusiast
Extrovert	Introvert
Married (3 times) Divorced (twice)	Married (3 times) Divorced (3 times)
Baby Boomer	Baby Boomer
Presbyterian Christian	Non-Denominational Christian (Baptist Family)
Reality Show Entertainer	Creative Artistic Entertainer (film, music, stage)
Best Selling Author	Prolific Author
Pro-Life (former pro-choice)	Pro-Life (former pro-abortion feminist)
Conservative (Republican)	Conservative (Frederick Douglass Republican)

One Blood ("We all bleed the same.")	One Blood/One Race (Acts 17:26; not color blind)
Parent and Grandparent	Parent and Grandparent
Loves America	Loves America

Following Trump from a Distance

The world took note of Donald J. Trump in the 1970's. For many, his larger than life lifestyle was intriguing. As one who was among the curious admirers of the young dynamo, I found myself following the daily reports of the man with business savvy and a magnetic personality. While never having the "claim to fame" in the category of what we called "jetsetters" in those days, I was living on the fringes of the glamorous rich and famous.

Having attained a modicum of fame and success as a member of the iconic "King Family," as well as being married to a wealthy and successful young physician, I found myself being lured towards the spotlights of the world; a world with Donald Trump at "center stage." I was part of the crowd of "star gazers" that watched Mr. Trump climb the pinnacles of celebrity.

My father the Rev. Dr. A. D. King, and my famous uncle, the Rev. Dr. Martin Luther King, Jr. had been killed in 1968 and 1969. At the beginning of the next decade, the world was in flux. The "Free Love

Movement" heralded a hedonistic wave of carnal and sensual pursuit of what some would consider to be pleasure. Ironically, this was the era that gave rise to what would become "The Trump Mystique."

In the early 1970's, before I became a born-again Christian in 1983, I must admit that I lived my life vicariously through watching people that I admired moving through their glittering lifestyles. During the first part of the decade, I was a young divorcee, mother of a young son, and a "rabid feminist." During those years, I experienced two abortions, a miscarriage, and divorce. Roe V Wade became law on my 22nd birthday; January 22, 1973.

During this time, Donald Trump was part of the world of the "rich and famous." He had an electrically magnetic personality, and was sought out by many who just wanted to be in his circle. The jetsetters appeared on television talk shows and on the cover of the popular magazines. As a young playboy millionaire, Mr. Trump was admired for his exploits during an age when "anything goes" ruled the day. He and those in his circles were looked up to as people many would want to be like. From a distance, Donald Trump appeared to be a force to be reckoned with. He was; and he still is.

In 1977, as the world watched, Donald Trump married the beautiful and intriguing super model Ivana Zeinickova. Ironically, I became a newlywed around that same time. Of course, that's where the similarities diverged. The famous Trump super couple was bathed in luxury, fame and fortune. I was pregnant, and my grandfather, Rev. Martin Luther King, Sr. insisted that there would be no more abortions. Granddaddy performed the "shotgun wedding" himself.

Even though our circumstances are very vastly different, and there was seemingly no connection between my life and the Trump Mystique, I still enjoyed watching from a distance as The Trump Family worked and played as the rest of the world went about the more mundane business of making ends meet. The Trumps had it all; marriage, family and money. Back then, that's how the "Trump Mystique" looked through my not so "rose colored glasses."

Over the next few years, my life accelerated. I began to "move up in the world." My second husband graduated from two intense programs, and became a licensed physician and an attorney at the same time. He was extremely successful, and began to make money right away. Together, we moved into the "upper echelon" of our world. During this time, I ran for political office, became a Georgia State Legislator, and also became a film and stage actress. As somewhat of a "power couple," we attained social status in our own little corner of the world. Still, somehow, I found time to monitor the Trump Trajectory, even though my own world was enlarging.

Looking back at what was happening in the world during those days, I'd have to say that nothing in life occurs by means of happenstance, or coincidence or as serendipity. In other words, everything happens for a reason. I say this because, for some reason, and I pray that I'm not being grandiose in my reasoning, for some reason I can empathize with the trajectory of President Trump's life, because in some ways, we seem to have been on a similar beaten path. Think about it. I entered into a marriage about the same time the President did. My seemingly successful marriage ended around the time the highly publicized marriage of Donald and Ivana Trump ended in a brutal divorce.

Over the next few decades, I, like President Trump, found myself married and divorced. He divorced two times; I divorced three times. Having experienced these heartbreaking traumas of having my life torn apart and my children scattered, I find myself very reluctant to cast any stones at President Trump for his so called "checkered past." I have been forgiven, healed and redeemed from so many hurts; yet I have also experienced many victories. I'm not alone in this journey. In retrospect, I truly believe that President Trump has experienced many more victories than I have.

Why Trump?

I admire President Trump for so many reasons. He is a family man. He's a successful business man. He is an active listener; and he is result driven. Interestingly enough, he seems to have always been that way. Of course, I only met President Trump in person in 2015. However, as I've said, I've watched and known him for many years, from a distance.

My favorite recollection of President Trump "back in the day," is when he was interviewed by Oprah Winfrey in 1988. During the interview, after listening to Businessman Trump's thoughts for making America better, Oprah asked the successful businessman if he would ever consider running for President of the United States. His answer was what I have become accustomed to thinking of as "classic Trumpian:"

"I'd make our allies pay their fair share. We're a debtor nation; something's going to happen over the next number of years in this country, because you can't keep going on losing $200 billion," he said on "The Oprah Show" back then. "We let Japan come in and dump everything right into our markets... They come over here, they sell their cars, their VCRs. They knock the hell out of our companies. And, hey, I have tremendous respect for the Japanese people. I mean, you can respect somebody that's beating the hell out of you, but they are beating the hell out of this country. Kuwait, they live like kings... and yet, they're not paying. We make it possible for them to sell their oil. Why aren't they paying us 25 percent of what they're making? It's a joke."

In response to his passionate and thoughtful discourse, Oprah said: "This sounds like political, presidential talk to me. I know people have talked to you about whether or not you want to run; would you ever?"

"Probably not," Mr. Trump replied. "But I do get tired of seeing the country get ripped off. I just don't think I have the inclination to do it. If it got so bad, I would never want to rule it out totally, because I really am tired of seeing what's happening with this country," Trump said. "We're really making other people live like kings, and we're not."

Then, President Trump spoke these iconic words: [If I did run] "I think I'd win," Trump said. "I'll tell you what: I wouldn't go in to lose." Spoken like the true icon many of us have grown to know and love. President Donald John Trump did run for the assignment of 45th President of the United States of America; and yes. He won.

Interestingly, before President Trump made his victorious bid in 2016, he spoke with Larry King in 1999. Then Businessman Trump told the then popular media mogul that he would choose Oprah Winfrey as his vice president if he ever made the run. Of course, since President Trump is a Republican and Oprah is a liberal, in the 2016 election, that didn't happen. After all, oil and water don't mix; and apples aren't oranges.

Why Trump?

What happened between 1988 and 2016? Why did President Donald John Trump give up his billionaire lifestyle to become humiliated, ridiculed and slandered in order to serve the American people? I've often wondered if maybe he's like so many of us that lived through the "topsy-turvey" Boomer era and have emerged on the other side with a burning desire to leave something of value to our children, grandchildren, and great grandchildren?

I dare say that life's ups and downs have affected President Trump in ways that have made him stronger. A weaker person could not have made it so far in life. A broken person could not stand up to the storms that President Trump and his family face every day.

I would also say that in many ways, I grew up watching President Donald John Trump from a distance. Somehow, just watching him move through life, with all of the ups and downs, without skipping a beat, was and still remains a source of encouragement to me. So, I guess it's fair to say that part of the answer to "Why Trump" for me is personal. POTUS has been a source of encouragement to many in times of transformation.

Why Trump?

When Black America loved Donald J. Trump

Oprah and Trump partied together at Tyson's 30thCredit
Getty – Contributor

When Black America loved Alveda C. King

Arm in arm march in honor of Martin Luther King Jr.'s
birthday, Tuesday, Jan. 15, 1985. (AP Photo/Ric Reld)

Table of Content

Why Trump?

INTRODUCTION

The year is 2020. Here in America, as I sit down to record and write about the days and times of President Donald J. Trump from an inside view, he is in the hospital battling COVID19. I am grateful to pray for President Trump as I finish this part of a journal of the journey. Please forgive me as I share this, testimony with you; I will repeat many experiences from the encounters, because they overlap in my mind, much like waves lap upon the shores of time.

In 2018 the thought came to me that I should and could write a book about President Trump. By that time, I had been to several meetings in the White House, and had not only met the President as a candidate; I had been invited into meetings with him in The White House.

I began sorting through photos, documents, my blogs, my calendar, and cataloguing in my mind a book that would become this journal. Early in the year, my friend Ginger Howard had a dream of us writing a book together. Through a miraculous series of events, Ginger and I began to write our book and seek a publisher. It was my hope that both books would become a package deal and we'd release them together. That didn't happen.

For several months, I laid this journal project aside, and went full steam ahead with Ginger on WE'RE

NOT COLORBLIND. It is now a bestseller, praise God.

A few weeks ago, here in 2020, God spoke to my heart. "Man said no to your book [about Trump.] I did not say no." That "word" was an epiphany for me. So, I got busy, and this book WHY TRUMP? is now a reality.

The journal is written in the format of a diary and a scrapbook, with short narratives and photos from my personal collection. A full photo gallery is available at www.whytrumpbook.com

This format is presented as my answer to the question that so many people have asked me so many times in regard to my prayers and support for our 45th President. Why Trump?

Thank you for your prayers and support as you read this book. God bless you.

A Bull in A China Shop

"During the first debate, I remember texting friends, 'Mr. Trump is like a bull in a china shop.' Then God revealed this to me. 'Yes, and bulls are beautiful and magnificent creatures, and china is fragile.'

"In context of America's economy, the bull represents a strong economy. Even in the face of COVID-19 and the street riots of 2020, we must remember we entered this era with a strong economy and the job rate for African Americans is the highest in recent history. And yes, the China issue is very fragile." – Evangelist Alveda King

On August 6, 2015, 24 million viewers tuned in to the GOP Presidential debate; I was in that number. There were 17 candidates in the race back then; that was before the field would be weeded down to ten. At the time, my short list of five picks from the hopefuls were Mr. Trump and Dr. Ben Carson tied at the top:

Why Trump?

- ✓ Donald Trump
- ✓ Ben Carson
- ✓ Mike Huckabee
- ✓ Marco Rubio
- ✓ Ted Cruz

Scott Walker

Jeb Bush

Rand Paul

Chris Christie

John Kasich

Meanwhile, it seemed as though America was holding her breath in anticipation of a coming transformation. Almost as if sensing that there was about to be a major upheaval amidst the norm, spirits of turbulence and unrest were growing in the nation.

I, along with millions of viewers, had my eyes glued to the "boob tube." I hadn't experienced this much anticipation over an election since the "hanging chad" days of George W. Bush. As each candidate spoke, I aligned my order of "favorites." Needless to say, at the end of the election, my two "favorites" came out on top, with President Trump the winner, and Secretary Carson as a strong cabinet member.

However, I'm getting ahead of the process. That night of the debate, with the top ten front runners on primetime television, Donald John Trump came out of the gate running hard and swinging harder. He was unique, he was bold and brash, and he reminded me of a "bull in a China shop." Even as I spoke the words out loud, saying he's like a bull in a china shop, I sensed the spirit of God speaking into my "inner ear" with a "still, small voice."

There was a quiet and powerful whisper. "Yes. And bulls are beautiful and magnificent creatures. And China is fragile."

I remember thinking – wow! I texted a prophetic friend with the message about the bull and china. He texted back: "Is the 'c' in china capital?" Wow again. China the nation is fragile. We can see that in the current revelations that COVID19 originated in China. Also, the negotiations with China that have ensued during President Trump's first four years have shown China in a different, and yes, fragile light.

Why Trump? He shines a light in corners others avoid.

Hello

First Trump/King Encounter in 2015

As the 2015-2016 presidential campaigns ensued, I still hadn't given a thought to meeting President Trump. On June 16, 2015 when POTUS announced his bid, just two days after his birthday, I was already on board praying with a group about Ben Carson's candidacy. Dr. Carson had announced his bid on May 4, 2015. On those early prayer calls, we were praying for a transition in our country, and asking God to guide our hearts and prayers by giving us a president who would help us return to God. Many of us on those calls wanted Ben Carson to be the chosen one.

Dr. Carson often joined the calls, and he would say: "God told me to run for president. God didn't say that I would be president." Of course, that went in one ear and out the other for many in the Carson camp. Having been elected to office and appointed by one president by then, I knew that nothing was guaranteed in politics. My mind and eyes were already on DJT as the next likely one that I would be blessed to support.

As I shared in the preface, for four and one-half decades, I admired and followed Donald John Trump from a distance. I never even tried to meet him, and didn't imagine I ever would. I was just content to watch and admire him from afar. As a young adult, before I became born again in 1983, I chased after a dream of becoming rich and famous. I followed the rich and beautiful avidly from a distance. That's how Donald Trump came to be on my radar. As a successful Georgia State Legislator and a budding stage and film actress, I was young and somewhat rich and famous myself in a small way. That state of being however, would not be my final destination.

After 1983, my focus shifted. I left politics and became a college professor. As a young wife and mother, and a newly born-again Christian, I began to chase after Jesus, almost fanatically in those days. It was around the time I was born again that I began to care less and less about the things of the world. Even though I had attained some fame in politics and the entertainment field, I was in a spiritual metamorphous, a transformational state.

However, one part of my former "star-seeking" mentality remained on my radar; the part of the world that centered on Donald J. Trump. Every now and then, when Trump the business mogul appeared in the news and popular magazines, his activities caught my attention. In the early 1990s, I was saddened to hear about "The Donald's" divorce from his first wife Ivana. I was going through a divorce myself at the time, and because I had a distant fondness for the Trump family by then, I sympathized from a distance.

Back then, I still had no dreams or aspirations of meeting Mr. Trump. While there were likely invisible paths that would converge, resulting in a meeting between the man who would one day become President of the United States, and the Christian Evangelist who was not yet even ordained, I couldn't see or imagine it. However, with God, nothing is serendipitous, or accidental, or happenstance. While neither of us knew it, Donald J. Trump would become President and Alveda King would become one of his "spiritual advisors." However, back then, we both had a long way to go, with hard choices to make along the way.

Why Trump?

In the late 1990s, as the world began looking towards the "turn of the century," and the millennial furor leaned towards fever pitch, there were transformations abounding. Donald Trump was again considering the world of politics as part of his roadmap. He was a favorite among the civil rights communities in those days; much celebrated by notables such as Al Sharpton and the liberal political and entertainment world.

In 1999, Trump spoke of his friend Oprah Winfrey as a potential vice-presidential candidate on a ticket with himself as the nominee for president. Of course, that didn't happen. As it turns out, Mr. Trump began to reveal that he had "conservative" leanings, and the warning flags began to go up. Interestingly, my trajectory was similar during those days. While in the seventies and early eighties I had been a Democrat and pretty much a social liberal, after 1983, my values began to refocus. I began to support a Bible world view, one that was more conservative in nature.

By the late 1990s, I had become a political "Independent." Gone was the liberal Democrat Georgia State Representative. She was replaced by "The Conservative King." In 1999, when Donald Trump discussed a political run for president as a conservative with Oprah Winfrey on his ticket, Alveda King left both the Democrat Party and the position as an independent voter, to become a "Frederick Douglass Republican." Consequently, as an African American conservative, I was among the twenty-first century African Americans who would be appointed in strategic administration positions during the George W. Bush presidential years.

Even though I didn't realize it then, my trajectory was being aligned with that of Mr. Donald J. Trump's. Over the next few years, I don't recall following the Trump trajectory as much as I had in previous times. However, I did note when his second marriage ended; my second marriage was over as well.

In the early part of the twenty-first century, I was divorced and then remarried for a third time. That short marriage ended in the first quarter of the first decade of century 21. During that time, people would make jokes about me competing with Elizabeth Taylor, saying my marriages didn't last as long as a pair of good shoes. That hurt; a lot. I've often wondered how President Trump has felt about his relationships over the years.

During the first decade of the 21st century, Donald Trump reached what many would consider to be the "prime years" of his life. Along the way, while expanding his already substantial dynasty, Mr. Trump married yet a third time. Some have said that the "third time is a charm." From my perspective, it is not good to compare his choices in mates. I am sure that each woman has her strengths and attractions. They all seem to be beautiful, intelligent and resilient. Who am I to judge anyone?

For the next few years, from the calendar years of 2000 to 2015, America elected two politically polar opposites as president; George W. Bush and Barack Hussain Obama. I voted for President Bush, and received my first presidential appointment from him. During the Obama years, I voted for Herman Cain and Mike Huckabee as write-in candidates.

I can only imagine that during those seasons, President Trump was already grappling with a decision of whether or not he would ever run for president. I had yet to meet him. I didn't even know anyone who was close enough to Mr. Trump to discuss whether his cryptic words from 1988 about winning if he should ever choose to win; or his thoughts about Oprah as a running mate, were foretelling a possible political race for him.

When President Trump did announce that he was running for president, I was as shocked as many were to hear this news. It was simply amazing. When he announced that he was running as a Republican, I was astonished. I hadn't done my homework. Before then, I had just assumed that because he was so popular with prominent liberals, he had to be a liberal as well.

Well, history has already recorded what happened next. Even as the candidates geared up for the 2016 presidential race, for the first time in four decades, the share of Americans living in middle-income households fell below 51 percent in 2015, according to an analysis of government data by the Pew Research Center.

In early 2015, according to Pew, the United States had 121.3 million adults in both lower- and upper-income households combined, compared with only 120.8 million in the middle-class. Inequality was increasing on opposite ends of the spectrum.

Gun deaths had become almost as common as traffic deaths in our communities. Global poverty was shifting. There were unforeseen shifts in migration arising. China ended its enforced "one child policy." Millennials replaced Boomers as America's largest generation. Same-sex marriage became legal according to common law in America.

Then in 2015, Donald J. Trump signed on to the very crowded and top heavy Republican political slate in one of the most highly contested presidential campaigns in history. There were seventeen Republican contenders that garnered notice. Mr. Trump stood out among the crowd. It was a "no holds barred" season for the man who would be the victor of that battle.

In the opening photo of this chapter, you can see the moment I met Candidate Trump, the presidential hopeful at a policy conference in November 2015. Father Frank Pavone and I stood in a long line to take photos with Mr. Trump and other presidential hopefuls. As I walked towards the soon to be president of the United States (though none of us knew that he would win at that time), I stretched out my hand in greeting. I remember starting to greet him, saying: Hello, I'm... I remember him laughing as I approached, and saying: "You don't have to tell me who you are. I know who you are. I like you." We both laughed, and shook hands. For a moment, time stood still. Then I said: I like you too.

Why Trump? From that day on, I have always remembered the sincerity of his words, and his many good deeds that have followed. Hello.

Black People, I want your vote.

ELECTIONS 2016
VIRGINIA BLACK MINISTERS ENDORSE TRUMP

President Trump makes many unprecedented and successful moves. In August of 2016, President Trump rocked the political world with his boldness by publicly addressing the elephant in America's living rooms with a very candid observation. Black Americans had been exploited by the Democrat Party and in more recent history, in a departure of the party of Lincoln, pretty much ignored by the Republican Party.

President Trump made a bold appeal. "Black people, I want your vote." He went on in classic Trumpian style, asking the question that many were likely thinking. "What [the h*ll] do you have to lose?"

Why Trump?

In response, I remember thinking this: Good question; but tell us also what we have to gain by voting for you.

Why Trump? Not only has President Trump shown us what we have to gain. In his 47 months of office, he has helped increase the gains to the Black community more than any other president has in decades.

What Do You have to GAIN?

"Look at how much African American communities have suffered under Democratic control," Candidate Trump said to his supporters. "To those hurting, I say, 'What do you have to lose by trying something new like Trump?' You're living in poverty, your schools are no good, you have no jobs, 58 percent of your youth are unemployed. What the [h*ll] do you have to lose?" Candidate Donald Trump, 2016

BLACK ECONOMIC EMPOWERMENT AND ACCESS TO CAPITAL

Jobs, Jobs, Jobs

- Reach even greater levels of historic employment and wage growth for the Black Community set in 2019, so that anyone looking for a job gets one
- Seek infrastructure funding that will lead to widespread growth in the annual $5000 federal contracting opportunities
- Grow minority owned businesses with additional tax cuts to stimulate hiring and investment
- Encourage onshoring and development of domestic manufacturing to increase supply chain business development and employment
- Examine barriers to employment including fees, occupational licensing, arrest record inaccuracy and expungement
- Increase activity in opportunity zones including benefits for local hires
- Invest almost $200 toward broadband and internet access to create job opportunities, improve classroom connectivity, and the ability to obtain tele-health services

Fueling Access To Capital For Black Owned Businesses

- Increase opportunities for small business lending and technical assistance through Community Development Financial Institutions, in order to grow business and create generational wealth opportunities with over $4000 in lending
- Examine alternative ways to build credit including rent, utilities, and phone bills
- Make the Minority Business Development Agency permanent, appoint its leader to the Assistant Secretary of Commerce level, create a sub-office of African American Affairs, and engage with private sector advisors to ensure real world plans and solutions
- Increase the number of Black owned contracting businesses, financial services entities, and private equity investment funds through regulatory reform and up to $40B in government funding alongside traditional private investment
- Advance lending relationships with financial institutions, particularly those businesses who weren't able to participate in PPP
- Host senior executives from major financial banks to advance new and equitable lending programs for black communities

MORE EDUCATION OPPORTUNITIES

Education African Americans Can Choose

- Federal, state, and local community partnership to close failing schools to replace with full school choice and education opportunity to put American parents back in control over their children's futures
- Increase childcare tax credits and provide greater access to quality pre-school

Education African Americans Can Afford

- Continue to protect the vital role of Historically Black Colleges & Universities
- Spur innovation ecosystems by connecting minority institutions with the Federal Government's broad range of scientific and engineering research and development
- Increase the amount of Pell grants and allow for vocational employment and second chance home comers
- Advance targeted apprenticeship and job training programs

BETTER AND CHEAPER HEALTHCARE

Affordable Care You Can Trust

- Reduce costs and improve access to quality healthcare through HRSA
- Deliver real price transparency so you know the costs before care is received
- Opportunity to be in charge of your own healthcare and choose your own doctor
- Eliminate Long Standing Healthcare Disparities
- Investments into the causes and cures of kidney disease, high blood pressure, diabetes, Sickle Cell Disease, maternal mortality, and other diseases that disproportionately affect African American populations
- Increase access to telemedicine and innovate technologies to empower patients with flexibility and tools for better health
- Public-Private Partnership to develop healthcare facilities in low-income areas
- Defend religious freedom exemptions to respect religious believers and always protect life

SAFETY & JUSTICE

Safe Streets

- Continue to make historic improvements to the criminal justice system through common sense actions like the First Step Act, including increase use of drug rehabilitation vs. drug incarceration
- Announce a National Clemency Program to unite families and revest in human potential, focusing on wrongful prosecution and rehabilitation
- Restore safety to American's great cities by working with police departments, community leaders and mental health professionals to install the most responsive, professional, and accountable models of policing, including diversity training and accreditation standards
- Advance second chance hiring to get rehabilitated citizens with a criminal record back on the job

Prosperous Black Communities

- Champion federal policy reforms to advance home ownership initiatives
- Partner with local leaders in black communities to ensure maximum federal support for neighborhood revitalization
- Make Juneteenth a National Holiday
- Prosecute the KKK and ANTIFA as terrorist organizations and make lynching a national hate crime
- Fuel black farmers and access to healthy foods to address food disparities
- Favorable trade deals to bring back manufacturing jobs and health black contractors, farmers, inventors, and consumers
- Defend religious liberty and African American churches that lift the conscience of our nation
- Collaborate with cities and counties to address mental illness and substance abuse

President Trump's Platinum Plan

As it turns out, the 45th President of the United States has a solid plan for including African Americans in the Make America Great Again platform. We have gained so much in this first four years. Why Trump? Many African Americans will be voting for President Trump in 2020 with the hopes and expectations of him finishing the fine job he has already started in his first four years.

Killing Babies is Wrong!

The photo above was taken after a call POTUS made to the prolife community. It was an honor for me to be in the Oval Office as part of a group invited to witness a phone call from President Trump to the prolife community. From day one, President Trump has been a champion of the unborn. Even during the debates, President Trump has remained a strong champion for life from the womb to the tomb.

Why Trump?

"If you go with what Hillary is saying, in the ninth month, you can take the baby and rip the baby out of the womb of the mother just prior to the birth of the baby." Donald Trump to Hillary Clinton in 2016 debate.

"In 2016 then-candidate Donald Trump's groundbreaking written commitments were instrumental to mobilizing pro-life voters to propel him to victory. During his first term, President Trump has become the most pro-life president our nation has ever seen. But there is more work to be done and that is why the pro-life movement is working vigorously to secure four more years for President Trump and Vice President Pence. President Trump's letter [to the prolife community] is further proof of pro-life momentum heading into this pivotal election, following the most explicitly pro-life Republican convention ever – in stark contrast to the Democrats who were too afraid to even utter the word 'abortion.' Joe Biden and Kamala Harris's support for abortion on-demand, paid for by taxpayers is extreme, immoral, and will prove to be a loser at the ballot box." Marjorie Dannenfelser, SBA List

On the other hand, the alternative in this 2020 election is simply unacceptable. President Trump's opponents on the Biden/Harris ticket support abortion throughout pregnancy; and they are flirting with infanticide beyond birth.

Why Trump? Life is a civil right. Abortion is a civil wrong. I'm prolife, and he's the most pro-life president ever.

We Will Say Merry Christmas Again!

Alveda and Son Eddie 2019, Christmas at The White House

After President Trump's prolife stance and his promise to protect the little babies in the womb, my next favorite promise that he made and has kept is "we will say Merry Christmas again." In 2015, when the campaigns for the office of 45th President of America began, Americans had all but abandoned the cheerful words "Merry Christmas" in the public marketplace. In the most extreme instances, employers were forbidding their staff to say those words to customers. Then, enter Candidate Donald J. Trump with the bold promise to America. I had the honor to be in the audience at a Trump Rally in 2016, when he promised members of the faith community gathered there: "We will say Merry Christmas again."

I, and family members and friends have been invited to the White House every Christmas since POTUS 45 took office. We entered the White House each time with the words "Merry Christmas" on our lips and joy in our hearts. At the White House, the beautiful decorations and hospitality have been impeccable each year; thanks to the marvelous planning and delivery of First Lady Melania Trump.

First Lady Trump has also graciously invited the children of our family and their parents to several Easter Egg Rolls; all lovely occasions. Then there have been the lovely dinners and receptions. Words just cannot describe the exquisite beauty, dignity and hospitality of these events.

Why Trump? He and his FLOTUS have made the White House a home to America. Merry Christmas [For me Happy Birthday Lord Jesus] and Happy Easter [For me Happy Resurrection] are alive and well in America again.

The Trump Diversity Coalition

Alveda, Bruce LeVell and Don, Jr.

In 2016, Dr. Ben Carson exited the Presidential Race and joined Candidate Donald J. Trump's campaign team. My friend Day Gardner and I immediately joined in with Dr. Carson, and we were embraced by the Trump National Diversity Coalition. Bruce LeVell, Executive Director of NDCT, Inc. became our mentor on the campaign trail. I was assigned the post of "spiritual advisor" for the group.

Why Trump? We had so much to gain.

He Won!
Praise the
Lord!

My First POTUS Prayer Meeting

January 21, 2017 – Washington National Cathedral

On their first official day in office, the very valiant and faithful President Trump and his graceful and gracious wife, Melania, along with the noble Vice President Mike Pence and his steadfast wife, Karen, were seated in the front row at Washington National Cathedral for the morning prayer service. This was the day after his inauguration; and the day before my birthday. The families of the first and second families were close by. I was among those honored to speak and pray at the occasion. None of us knew what lay ahead of us. We were all moving forward in faith. What stands out most in my memory of that day was the diversity of the congregation; and the tears flowing down the face of FLOTUS.

Why Trump?

WHY TRUMP? In his inauguration speech the day before, and his presence at a prayer meeting the day after, President Trump set the tone for our nation to pray for the days ahead.

Religious Freedom

May 4, 2017

"America is a nation of believers, and together we are strengthened by the power of prayer. Religious freedom, America's first freedom, is a moral and national security imperative. Religious freedom for all people worldwide is a foreign policy priority of the United States, and the United States will respect and vigorously promote this freedom." ~President Donald J. Trump

On May 4, 2017, President Donald J. Trump signed an Executive Order promoting Free Speech and Religious Liberty. This is the day I received my first presidential pen.

On May 3, 2018 President Donald J. Trump signed another Executive Order to ensure that the faith-based and community organizations that form the bedrock of our society have strong advocates in the White House and throughout the Federal Government. With this Executive Order President Trump declaring the effort to protect religious freedom as both a domestic and foreign policy priority.

On June 2, 2020, he signed the executive order on Advancing International Religious Freedom. President is dauntless in his commission to Make America Great Again, and to be a force for good around the world. Foremost, his success in bringing understanding and sanity to the situation regarding Israel is unprecedented.

Why Trump? Even though there is an ongoing resistance whose goal is to staunch our religious liberty, President Trump is standing in leadership, fighting for America's right to worship freely.

First Step Act

On December 21, 2018, while Congress debated the merits of funding a 2,000-mile wall along the U.S. southern border, I and other supporters of the criminal justice reform act had the honor of standing beside the president as he signed into law the First Step Act, a bipartisan overhaul of the criminal justice system that will give judges more sentencing flexibility, especially for nonviolent drug crimes. It was a remarkable day. Ja'Ron looked so happy. I received yet another historical presidential pen. It was just the perfect time also to encourage the president to ignore haters and build the wall.

Why Trump? He has "true grit." Also, he delivers on his promises.

MLK Park

Alveda, cousin Isaac Newton Farris, Jr. and Bruce LeVell witness signing of MLK National Park Act. (January 8, 2018)

Words just cannot express how blessed we were this day. We were on Airforce One. President Trump signed the bill which had been co-sponsored by the late Congressman John Lewis. The new law expanded an existing historic site commemorating my uncle, MLK. And yes, I received another presidential pen.

Then we were invited by the president to join him in his ground transportation, a huge hybrid of tank and SUV, nicknamed "The Beast," to attend the college football championship game.

Why Trump?

At the game, we held our breaths to see if the players would kneel or stand for the National Anthem, because there was a heated debate surrounding recent protests over the matter.

Why Trump? Another unforgettable moment in a series of many blessed events in the Days and Times of President Donald J. Trump.

With President Trump at the NCAA Championship Game

The Round Tables

There have been many visits to the White House for me during the first term of President Donald J. Trump. Shortly after the Inauguration, Father Frank Pavone and I visited the office of FLOTUS to deliver a prayer blanket. She wrote a lovely thank you letter to the woman who lovingly crafted that blanket. Over time, I've been invited to policy meetings, receptions, dinners, and the like. The Round Table meetings always take on a life of their own.

The round table meetings in the "war room" just outside the Oval Office have been remarkable. Whether I was attending in February for Black History Month with key black leaders, or in summer with a diverse group of pastors and leaders, I am always blessed when POTUS enters the room from his Oval Office. It is during those times that I see firsthand how the media deliberately misleads the American public. They accuse President Trump of being self-centered and domineering. Nothing can be further from the truth.

In each meeting, once seated, POTUS is an active listener; engaged and engaging; warm and interactive. Each time, he turns to each person present, invites attendees to take the floor, and he listens. His responses are always shorter than expected; yet they are very insightful and promising.

Why Trump?... because he is a participative leader.

Trump Prayers

Alveda with Rev. Owens, Rev. Nelson, and Bishop Jackson

In the photo above, I am outside the White House with three pastors and national leaders; Rev. Bill Owens, Rev. Dean Nelson, and Bishop Harry Jackson. Each of us has national and global platforms. We had just attended a round table meeting with President Trump.

We had also prayed with the President. In the photo below, I am on the platform with other pastors and leaders, and led by Pastor Paula White, the president's pastor, we are praying for POTUS.

In every meeting I have attended with President Trump, he has welcomed prayer. As a prayer partner to the White House, and spiritual advisor to Black Voices for Trump, I can't say enough about the importance of prayer in government.

Why Trump? I am very grateful to President Trump who says: "We don't worship government; we worship God.

Black History at The White House

It has been an honor for me to be invited to Black History events and discussions throughout President Trump's administration. In February 21, 2017, we joined President Trump for a visit to the Smithsonian's National Museum of African American History and Culture. Secretary Ben Carson and Senator Tim Scott were among those present. We spent time at several of the exhibits; the Frederick Douglass presentation was one of them. I was later appointed to the Frederick Douglass Bicentennial Commission by President Trump.

Why Trump?

I selected the photo above because it is the most recent Black History engagement with our president. On February 23, 2019, POTUS not only hosted a Round Table session at The White House, with several leaders, as you see pictured above. Following that meeting, we all joined a much larger group and the president spoke openly regarding COVID19 and the ramifications. The president chose to encourage us, rather than scare us.

Why Trump? He is working with us, and with God's guidance, he is leading America through the troubled waters before us.

Still Not Racist

SCAN ME

www.stillnotracist.com

During his first four years, President Trump has done more for Black Americans than other presidents have done in decades. His plans that include incentives such as Opportunity Zones, Farmers to Family, Jobs, Housing, Health Care and Life, Support for Israel and Africa, Juneteenth; all are beneficial in some shape, form or fashion, to all Americans.

Trump Presidential Score Card: A+

✓   **ENTREPRENEURSHIP**

Black Americans are seeing unprecedented levels of economic success with record low unemployment rates, more jobs, and higher incomes:

• Over 1.4 million more Black Americans have found a job since President Trump's election

• Black unemployment reached a historic low

• President Trump designated 8,760 Opportunity Zones that are projected to spur $100 billion in private investment in minority communities

• The Trump administration established a fund to deploy $1 billion in capital funding for minority-owned businesses through the Commerce Department

• The Black poverty rate is now at its lowest level in history

✓ **SCHOOL CHOICE**

President Trump called on Congress to pass school choice legislation to expand educational opportunities for all American children, especially those in our nation's inner cities:

• President Trump's 2020 budget called for $500 million in federal funding for school choice, and in 2018 he signed legislation increasing school choice funding by $42 million

• His Administration proposed the Education Freedom Scholarships and Opportunity Act

✓ **HISTORICALLY BLACK COLLEGES AND UNIVERSITIES**

President Trump restored funding and increased investment for HBCUs by 14 percent:

• Provided more than $500 million in loans to HBCUs through the Capital Financing Program

• Worked with HBCUs to protect $80 million in Title III carryover funding

• Signed the FUTURE Act into law, which permanently funds HBCUs and simplifies the FAFSA application

• In 2018, President Trump signed a budget deal which forgave more than $300 million in debt owed by four HBCUs impacted by natural disasters and provided $10 million in loan payment deferments for schools that face financial difficulties, including HBCUs

• President Trump worked with Congress to lift the ban on Pell Grants on summer classes

✓ **CRIMINAL JUSTICE REFORM**

President Trump signed the historic FIRST STEP ACT into law:

• 90 percent of those who have had their sentences reduced are Black Americans

• FIRST STEP ACT shortens mandatory minimum sentence for nonviolent drug crimes

• The law allows offenders sentenced under racially motivated mandatory minimums to petition for revaluation

Why Trump?

- President Trump launched the "Ready to Work" Initiative, which helps released prisoners gain meaningful employment
- President Trump has proposed the Second Step Act to partner with corporate America to create opportunities for former prisoners to rejoin society

Why Trump? Our president has said "we all bleed the same." We are One Blood, One Human Race, One America, and with the help of God, under the leadership of President Trump, we as a people are moving ahead with dignity, in faith; together.

March for Life

As a mother who has survived, repented, and been forgiven by God for the experiences of aborting two babies, and a miscarriage due to damage from those abortions; as Executive Director of Civil Rights for The Unborn for Priests for Life; and as a Christian Evangelist; words cannot express how humbled I was to stand behind Donald J. Trump, the 45th President of the United States of America at the Annual March for Life in Washington, D. C.

Why Trump? Because he is the most prolife President ever.

The Pardon

(Excerpts from Newsmax article by David Patton dated
February 19, 2020)

*When best-selling author and BET reality TV star
Angela Stanton-King received word on Tuesday that
President Trump had just granted her a full pardon,
she was literally overcome.*

*"I just started hyperventilating right at the airport,"
she told Newsmax. "I was just crying like a baby.
People thought someone had died."*

*"I just wanted to finally, truly be free. Today, hours
before my birthday, it has happened for me ... and I'm
still in absolute disbelief, I'm in shock."*

Why Trump?

There had been hints something was coming. Her longtime mentor, evangelist and Newsmax Insider Alveda King, the executive director of civil rights for the unborn with Priests for Life, had received a call a few days before from a senator informing her the president was working on Stanton-King's pardon.

Then on Tuesday morning, the Alveda King Ministries founder was relaxing on her couch when she got a phone call.

"Could you take a call from the President of the United States?" the voice on the other end asked.

The niece of Rev. Martin Luther King Jr. replied "Well, I'm fainting right now."

The president said hello.

"Oh my gosh Mr. President," she joked, "I need to get up off the floor, I just passed out."

They shared a laugh and Trump said he was preparing a full pardon for Stanton-King.

Alveda King -- no relation -- considers Stanton-King her godchild in the sense that "God sent her to me, to guide and to help and to mentor."

President Trump asked Alveda, 'Is she a good person?"

The evangelist and pro-life warrior immediately replied, "Yes sir, really she is."

Why Trump?

"Good," said Trump, "because I'm signing this pardon right now…"

[Alveda said] "Wow, you really make promises, then you keep them."

"You get that," Trump answered. "Everybody doesn't, but you get it."

For Stanton-King, the pardon represented another amazing chapter in her life's extraordinary journey.

With Alveda King's help, Stanton-King [has] defied the odds. She went on to write a best-selling book about her journey, Life of a Real Housewife. The book launched her career as a publishing entrepreneur, and that led to a big role in a BET reality TV show. She also founded the American King Foundation, a nonprofit focused on criminal-justice reform and reuniting families that have been separated by mass incarceration.

Along with record employment for the African-American community, Trump is making good on his promise to enact criminal-justice reform. In December 2018, he signed off the First Step Act criminal justice reform bill. Another bill, the Next Step Act, is in the works to help people find employment once they've paid their debt to society.

"His works are speaking for him now," Stanton-King said. "People are seeing results, and with the First Step Act we have many of our fathers and our

brothers and our uncles coming home from prison, and they're not being shy about it: They're like, 'You know, Trump did this for us.'"

Trump's outreach to African-American voters appears to have caught the political left flatfooted. After the news of Tuesday's pardons broke, several progressives fired off statements offering familiar talking points that seemed strangely out-of-touch.

[An] obvious implication [from the left]: That Trump was only pardoning white people.

Stanton-King soon tweeted back a two-word response, "I'm BLACK." And Katrina Pierson, a senior adviser to Trump's 2020 campaign, jumped in as well, citing a Sentencing Project study that found over 90 percent of those resentenced under the First Step Act were African-American.

[In 2019] Stanton-King said she [was] getting 10 or 12 messages a day from people in her community telling her they've decided to vote for Trump. [That number has multiplied significantly since then.]

"There are a lot of people who may not be saying it vocally or using their platforms for it, but they're saying it behind closed doors and they're all going to secretly vote for him," she told Newsmax.

[Stanton King] also predicted that Trump "is going to do very, very well this election, I have absolutely

no doubt about it. People are waking up, and they're seeing it. I'm seeing it right before my eyes."

Currently, here in 2020, Angela Stanton King is a candidate for U. S. Congress for the 5th District seat, formerly held by civil rights activist John Lewis.

Why Trump? Jesus came to set the captives free. God is moving in these days; President Trump is praying with us, and God is guiding us.

Angela and Alveda at The White House

47

Honors for My Daddy

Secretary Bernhardt signs the designation for
the A.D. King Home. Photo by Tami A.
Heilemann, Interior.

On September 24, 2020, U.S. Secretary of the Interior
David L. Bernhardt was joined by Naomi Ruth
Barber King, who is the wife of Alfred Daniel (A.D.)
King, Dr. Alveda King, who is the daughter of A.D.
King, Omie Crockett, who is the owner of A.D. King
home, Jacqueline Washington Crockett, who is the
daughter of Omie Crockett, and other distinguished
guests at the Reverend A.D. King, Sr. house as he
signed a proclamation designating the home to be
included in the African American Civil Rights
Network (AACRN). This designation further recognizes
A.D. King's numerous contributions to advance civil
rights as the leader of the Birmingham Campaign.

"President Trump worked with Congress to establish
the American Civil Rights Network to remember and

tell the complete story of the struggle for civil rights to foster healing, tolerance and understanding among all Americans," said Secretary Bernhardt. "The King family endured incredible hardships in the fight for equality. This home is an important chapter in the story that has shaped American history. It is a chapter that will forever be told. The legacies of the King and Crockett families are powerful reminders of our continued efforts to create a more perfect union. It is my honor to add the A.D. King house to the African American Civil Rights Network."

Thank you, President Trump.

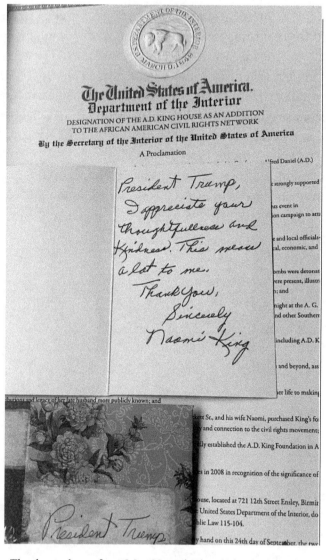

Thank you letter from Mrs. Naomi King (Alveda's Mother)

Selected Journal Entries

Thursday, 24 Sep 2020 1:35 PM

The home of the Rev. A.D. King that was firebombed in Birmingham, Alabama, on May 11, 1963 while he, and we, his family, were inside has been added to the African American Civil Rights Network.

My daddy, the Rev. A.D. King, is the brother of the Rev. Martin Luther King Jr. They live in heaven now.

Our former home at 721 12th Street in the Ensley section of Birmingham was added to the National Register of Historic Places in 2008 in recognition of Daddy's civil rights activism.

On Thursday, Sept. 24, the house will officially be included on the African American Civil Rights Network to ensure the history of the home and the legacy of its occupants are never forgotten.

Looking back on that Saturday night when our home was bombed in 1963, the night before Mother's Day, I can only thank God for those of our family who remain today.

That night, my dad was in the bedroom working on his sermon for the next day. My mother, Naomi Ruth Barber King, had just finished setting the table for Mother's Day dinner the next day. My brother was in the den watching a war movie; and the rest of us, my four siblings and I, were all in bed when the first bomb went off. It was a small bomb that only cracked the picture window at the front of the house.

At that time Daddy went to the front of the house where he saw Mama standing by the window. He told her, "Come on, it's too quiet out there," and he grabbed her hand and hurried her towards the back of the house. When we were about halfway to the back of the house, a second bomb exploded. The only thing that was left unbroken in the debris was a picture of Jesus.

Mama always says that the first bomb was designed to draw everyone to the front of the house, so the second bomb would kill us.

It was only by the Grace of God that no one was killed.

Daddy directed us to safety through the garage. Once outside, we climbed a fence to get away, fearing more explosions. I remember tearing my blue and white corduroy bathrobe, a gift from my grandmother, as we scaled the fence.

Back then, our home was the parsonage for the First Baptist Church of Ensley, where Daddy was pastor. When a crowd gathered after the explosions, Daddy climbed up on a car to ask people not to respond to violence with more violence, but to go home and pray.

Fr. Frank Pavone, National Director of Priests for Life, and Janet Morana, co-founder of Silent No More visited the house with me almost 20 years ago.

Why Trump?

"I have been to this house with Alveda, and have discussed with her many times the memories and lessons we can learn from it. The message of nonviolence is one that we are proud to carry forward and apply to our times," said Fr. Pavone.

Daddy not only worked alongside my Uncle M.L., but was a leader in his own right. When we moved to Kentucky for my father to take over Mount Zion Church in Louisville, Daddy also formed the Kentucky Christian Leadership Conference. He also led the Fair Housing Movement there. Subsequently, his office was bombed.

Daddy's death in 1969, falsely attributed to suicide and later to accidental drowning, was another assassination in our family. A week after he walked me down the aisle, he was killed. Now, years later, this tribute helps us to remember his legacy. We are grateful.

Why Trump?

Friday, 28 Aug 2020 12:11 PM

Today, Aug. 28, 2020 marks the 57th anniversary of the "I Have A Dream" speech delivered by the Rev. Dr. Martin Luther King, Jr., in front of the Lincoln Memorial in Washington, D.C. in 1963.

As we reflect on those tumultuous days of the 1960s, marked by race wars and street riots, some may wonder *what, if anything, has changed.*

Today as we remember the life, legend and legacy of Reverend Dr. Martin Luther King Junior, I'd like to revisit the iconic check marked insufficient funds he spoke about. This bounced check represents an injustice in the American Dream; a slight to the dignity of what was then known as the negro community.

That bounced check represents an injustice of the American Dream; a slight to the dignity of what was then known as the negro community.

Throughout America's history, Americans of African descent have been enslaved in the past, and are sometimes treated as second class citizens. This is so even in the America of today.

Translation? Meaning? Promises made, promises broken.

Today, if we are to believe the reports from the African American community, most recently by voices from Blacks associated with both the

Why Trump?

Democratic and Republican parties, during the RNC Convention, there is light on the horizon.

U.S. President Donald John Trump has made and kept many promises; including making good the check to Historically Black Colleges and Universities (HCBU), making good those opportunities for paychecks with an increase in the number of jobs for African Americans.

Our nation's 45th commander-in-chief has also brought about the return of nonviolent offenders to grateful families and communities.

With his Make America Great Again (MAGA) strategy, President Trump, with promises made and promises kept, and his reminder that we must worship God and not government, has produced great gains on behalf of the African-American community — and for all Americans — making good on the American dream for *all* Americans.

Now is the time, on this, the anniversary of "I Have a Dream," to raise our voices in unity.

Concurrently, we must decry all violence and injustice.

Dr. King once declared, "Injustice anywhere is a threat to justice everywhere."

Thus — to fix that which is broken in our troubled society:

—*Police brutality must cease*

—*Mob and gang violence must cease*

Why Trump?

—There must be a real and unified war on poverty

—Abortion and the war on the womb must cease

—The fight against religious freedom must cease

—The fight against the nuclear family must cease

Let us not also forget that human dignity matters and that God's love matters!

As Dr. King also stridently and rightfully observed, "We must learn to live together as brothers," and I add, as sisters, "or perish together as fools."

My brothers and sisters, we are one blood, one human race living in the United States.

We have so much to gain. We are not colorblind. We see clearly that skin color denotes ethnicity, not race. As one blood, one race, let us rise up and live.

The dream of the Rev. lives on and will grow into greater reality as we pray and work together.

Breaking News: Jacob Blake should not be shackled. He is a human being. And *non-violent* protests from athletes should be heard.

Injustice anywhere is a threat to justice everywhere.

How is a Black man shackled to a hospital bed a threat; but a white man shooting at protesters is not? *Answers please.*

Why Trump?

Written **Tuesday, 30 Jun 2020 2:41 PM**

Updated October 12, 2020

America needs constitutional justices like Amy Barrett. In a unique turn of events, she's President Trump's newest nominee. We are praying she takes a seat on the SCOTUS.

The Supreme Court's decision in the June Medical Services case totally disregards two classes of American people; the unborn and the women harmed by abortion. As someone who has had the misfortune of experiencing abortion, I am part of the Silent No More Campaign.

As a spokesperson for our awareness campaign, I joined hundreds of women hardened by abortion as we raised our voices to the Supreme Court in this case in an amicus brief, and we made clear that the abortionists who went to court to strike down this law are not the ones who are qualified to speak for women. On the contrary, we understand that laws are needed to protect women against an unscrupulous and unregulated abortion industry.

Abortion not only killed our children; it wounded us. That's why Louisiana, and every other state, has the right to pass laws that are meant to protect both us and our babies. The Supreme Court does women a disservice by striking down this law. Please visit Prolife Praise Variety Show for upcoming reports on the "civil wrong" aspects of abortion.

Why Trump?

My colleague Janet Morana, co-founder of Silent No More (a joint project of Priests for Life and Anglicans for Life) agrees: At Supreme CourtVictory.com.

You can read our amicus brief, and the many other briefs that were submitted, which show that the abortionists do not have a "close relationship" with the women who get abortions. They are, rather, strangers, who do not have their best interests at heart. As dissenting opinions in today's case stated, if someone wants to challenge this law in the lower courts, it should be someone who is actually injured by it. We know women are injured by abortion every day in this country. To read their stories, go to AbortionTestimonies.com."

My colleague Fr. Frank Pavone, National Director of Priests for Life, adds, "We respect the state legislators of Louisiana and of so many other states who are doing what the Courts have already said they can do, namely, pass laws regulating abortion in order to protect the health and safety of women. Louisiana did that well in this case. The Supreme Court should not be asked to second-guess the judgment of the state legislature as to what will help the women of their state. The Courts have a role to judge the constitutionality of laws, not their wisdom."

To see how our efforts are working, please visit End Abortion.US. The abortion rate in America is the lowest it has been since Roe v. Wade 410 U.S. 113 (1973), and in recent years states have passed more than 400 laws to protect the unborn. The number of freestanding abortion clinics in the U.S. has dropped from 2179 in 1991 down to 710 today. Additionally, President Trump has placed 200 anti-abortion judges on the federal bench.

Friday, 19 Jun 2020 4:47 PM

Happy Juneteenth everyone. My prayer today is that repentance, jubilee and Juneteenth will meet in a glorious trajectory of redemption.

Juneteenth marks the day in 1865 when people held as slaves in Texas finally learned that the abhorrent practice had ended two years previously, when President Abraham Lincoln signed the Emancipation Proclamation.

The proclamation freed "all persons held as slaves" in the states that had rebelled against the Union, and Texas was one of them. To understand how it took more than two years for slaves in Texas to learn they were free, you have to know a little bit of history about the Lone Star State.

Before Texas was a state, it was ruled by Spain and later, Mexico.

Both governments encouraged the freeing of slaves, but in the 1820s, when slave owners from the Southern states began migrating to Texas to grow cotton, the number of slaves began to grow. When Texas won its independence from Mexico in 1836, slavery was written into the new republic's constitution.

In 1845, when Texas was annexed to the U.S., there were some 30,000 slaves in the state.

By 1850, that number had jumped to more than 50,000.

Ten years later, the slave population numbered more than 180,000.

Texas seceded from the Union in 1861 and joined the southern confederacy. At that point, almost one-quarter of Texas families owned at least one slave. Following the Emancipation Proclamation of 1863, southern slaveholders began moving their human captives into Texas, where few Union soldiers were stationed, and the proclamation could be ignored.

That changed on June 19, 1865, when Maj. Gen. Gordon Granger and 2,000 Union soldiers arrived in Galveston and declared all slaves free by reading this proclamation:

"The people of Texas are informed that in accordance with a Proclamation from the Executive of the United States, all slaves are free. This involves an absolute equality of rights and rights of property between former masters and slaves, and the connection heretofore existing between them becomes that between employer and hired laborer."

A year later, Juneteenth celebrations began across Texas and eventually would pop up in other parts of the South. The Civil Rights movement in the 1950s and 1960s spread awareness of the holiday.

On April 4, 1968, my uncle, the Rev. Dr. Martin Luther King Jr. was assassinated in Memphis, Tennessee, in the midst of planning the Poor People's Campaign, which was to culminate in a peaceful march in Washington, D.C. Its purposes was to call on the government to address the housing and employment needs of all indigent people in the nation.

The campaign ultimately continued, and the Poor People's March took place on Juneteenth.

People from all over the country gathered in our nation's capital that day, and when they left, many of them took a newfound knowledge of and respect for the holiday with them.

Celebrations began springing up in other parts of the country.

My family has always celebrated Juneteenth.

Texas declared Juneteenth an official state holiday in 1980 and now, 46 states and the District of Columbia have some kind of observances.

But somehow, the holiday has remained a well-kept secret.

My colleague Janet Morana, executive director of Priests for Life, was a New York City public school teacher in an urban school, and even she had never heard of Juneteenth until I came to work for Priests for Life as director of Civil Rights for the Unborn in 2003.

This year, things have changed for the better for this holiday.

Amid the Black Lives Matter protests, President Trump's campaign inadvertently scheduled his first post-pandemic rally on June 19. When some black leaders asked him to change the date, our president was happy to do so, and it was widely reported in the media.

Now Juneteenth is on the national radar, and that's a good thing. All of us can stand to brush up on our history and this date is too important to be forgotten.

Some major companies, like the NFL and Nike, are making it a formal holiday.

I think it's time to go further and make it a national holiday. While statues of Confederate generals and racist officials are being toppled all over the country, we can never erase our painful past with regard to slavery.

What we can and should do, as Americans of every color, is celebrate slavery's end.

"The people that walked in darkness have seen a great light: they that dwell in the land of the shadow of death, upon them hath the light shined." - Isaiah 9:2 KJV

Tomorrow I will join thousands in Tulsa, OK to pray for President Trump and our nation. My prayers continue to be for repentance, redemption, and unity. May Repentance, Jubilee, Revival and Restoration converge! Let us, as one blood, with eyes wide open, (not colorblind), press on to victory.

Why Trump?

Wednesday, 17 Jun 2020 1:40 PM

"I prayed for freedom for twenty years, but received no answer until I prayed with my legs." — Frederick Douglass

"To all of the hurting families, I want you to know that all Americans mourn by your side. Your loved ones will not have died in vain. We're one nation, we grieve together, and we heal together. I can never imagine your pain or the depth of your anguish. But I can promise to fight for justice for all of our people." — President Donald J. Trump

Thanks to President Trump, his newest transformational executive order is bringing hope and sanity to the nation.

The Safe Policing for Safe Communities Act, which bans law enforcement from using chokeholds, will help deescalate the senseless slaughter and violence ravaging our communities.

Thus, President Trump elaborated yesterday:

"Under the executive order I'm signing today, we will prioritize federal grants from the Department of Justice to police departments that seek independent credentialing certifying that they meet high standards . . . As part of this new credentialing process, choke holds will be banned, except if an officer's life is at risk."

Along with this measure of intervention, the president has again shown leadership by continuing to host listening sessions regarding race relations. Due to these interactions, a major awareness of Juneteenth, a heretofore often overlooked holiday, is at the forefront.

This **history lesson** is good for America.

We are grateful for President Trump's leadership and sensitivity.

Another bright spot on the horizon is the Department of Justice's announcement of the launch of the Civil Rights Reporting Portal.

This new online tool will make it easier for the public to report a civil rights violation.

"The department is committed to upholding the civil and constitutional rights of all people in the United States," said Assistant Attorney General Eric Dreiband of the Civil Rights Division. Mr. Dreiband added, "The Civil Rights Reporting Portal will make it easier for the public to connect with us, which in turn makes us more effective at upholding these important rights. I encourage the public to use this portal to report civil rights violations."

As Americans, we should be very encouraged by these reports.

Meanwhile, we must continue to pray, to love, to forgive, and protest peacefully. We can peacefully protest by voting for candidates who support the sanctity of life, and the dignity of the one blood human race.

We are not colorblind. We can end the race wars by opening our eyes, seeing each other clearly as human beings; not separate races. We can learn to live together as brothers and sisters; not perish together as fools.

Let us continue to pray for our president and all of our leaders.

Why Trump?

Saturday, 30 May 2020 6:38 AM

I was very restless in my spirit yesterday. With my goddaughter, Angela Stanton King, "boots on the ground" in Minneapolis, Minnesota, COVID-19. Qualms are at critical mass. Personal family matters and that type of thing are weighing on my mind.

Yes, it was hard to pray — yet I did.

This morning as I spoke with Angela by telephone. The president's text about looting and shooting has surfaced. With my heart heavily grieved and moved by the cruel murder of George Floyd, who was a man of God, and other related events, an urgent cry arose in my heart.

Pray for an end to the looting and shooting. Please unite in prayer as one)

"And He has made from one blood every nation of men to dwell on all the face of the earth, and has determined their pre appointed times and the boundaries of their dwellings, so that they should seek the Lord, in the hope that they might grope for Him and find Him, though He is not far from each one of us; for in Him we live and move and have our being, as also some of your own poets have said, 'For we are also His offspring.'" – Acts 17:26-28 NKJV

I am saddened, yet remain undaunted that a quote of my uncle, the Rev. Dr. Martin Luther King, Jr., is being taken out of context:

Why Trump?

"Violence is the language of the unheard." Prophet Martin Luther King Jr. MLK spoke those words in defense of non-violence; he refused to promote violence as a solution to the ills of society.

As we are in "the eye of the storm," the solution remains: *Peace be still.*

We are in a state of flux. This is especially true with respect to George Floyd, The Rev. Dr. Martin Luther King, Jr., COVID-19, and the unborn aborted babies.

All of these issues now whirl around in one large chaotic storm. *Peace be still.*

Now more than ever, we must anchor with the Gospel of Jesus Christ.

I have said, "When and where peripherals collide, convergence is imminent."

Today, as the multiple storms of our time converge, what can we do so that we are not so fearful; so that we do not panic — but pray, believe, and love?

We must unite as one nation and one human race in constant prayer.

As I write this message, I am joining a business empowerment round table discussion with Vice President Mike Pence, Housing and Urban Development (HUD) Secretary Dr. Ben Carson, Georgia Governor Brian P. Kemp, the U.S. Secretary of Agriculture Sonny Perdue, Unity Bank officials — and others. It's all very encouraging.

Why Trump?

Thank God for promises made and promises kept. We must press on.

As we pray, as we thank God, as we see all of the progress we are making together in America, we will get through this. Pray for America.

Why Trump?

At best, Mothers' Day is always a poignant occasion; some are honoring elderly parents and remembering deceased mothers. If you're like me, many can't even physically attend regular church services with our parents and families due to COVID19.

Thank God for digital access to things that matter most.

Recently, with COVID19 looming globally, and in America with constant threats of more "race wars" abounding, almost everyone, me included, opens with "are you safe?"

Inadvertently we find ourselves ending our conversations and encounters with "Stay safe."

Today, while the news is of filled with the COVID-19 pandemic, please let's try to remember to be faith-filled rather than fearful — replacing panic with prayer.

The late evangelist, the Rev. Billy Graham once said that "We need a God Pill."

I couldn't agree more.

Thanks be to God, we still live in a Great and Praying America.

Here in Georgia, and echoing nationally, is the outcry against yet another racially motivated crime against humanity with the brutal murder of Ahmaud Arbery.

Why Trump?

I find myself listening over and over to the 30 second message of "One Blood" by my uncle, the Rev. Dr. Martin Luther King, Jr.

Dr. King was right. "We must learn to live together as brothers [and sisters], or perish together as fools."

We really are one human race, one blood, as according to Acts 17: 26-28 in scripture.

Neither are we color blind.

We can learn to live and love our neighbors as ourselves — with our eyes wide open.

Let us be grateful that our president and many Americans have not bowed, nor bent our knees to Baals. Crimes against humanity are being exposed as the swamp continues to be drained. ("We don't worship government, we worship God." – President Donald J. Trump.)

A few days ago, my 88-year-old mother showed me her application for an absentee ballot.

According to her, senior citizens are courted by political agents during election seasons.

Thus, gifts of food, transportation, and other favors are offered in the guise of helping our senior citizens. Dr. Ken Blackwell writes of an underlying motive of political agents who reach out to our seniors with great persuasion, in an attempt to sway votes, with pay-to-play.

Why Trump?

In recent a recent opinion piece, Dr. Ken Blackwell observed, "Yet the sacred right of today's seniors to have their political choices honored at the ballot box are at high risk because of vote fraud."

So, while I'm celebrating Mothers' Day with my mother, I'm also praying that her vote won't be violated.

In case you missed it, see my Mothers' Day show, first broadcast on EndAbortion.TV.

"Your eyes are windows into your body. If you open your eyes wide in wonder and belief, your body fills up with light. If you live squinty-eyed in greed and distrust, your body is a dank cellar. If you pull the blinds on your windows, what a dark life you will have!" – Matthew 6:22-23 MSG.

Thursday, 23 Apr 2020 10:04 AM

Friends, faith over fear and prayer over panic remain important as we love our neighbors as ourselves in this COVID19 battle. We are winning the fight. God is with us.

As we continue the POTUS led successful national efforts to curb COVID19's impact, we must continue to watch and pray. While as a Georgian, I understand Governor Kemp's decision on a gradual progression on opening up some of the small businesses, we must use wisdom as we prepare to venture out.

For example, you can go to Costco, Sam's, Publix, Kroger and all the major retail grocery stores etc. and see thousands of people in and out daily . . . But when you take a small business owner who has two or three employees and maybe have three or four customers a day, the small business owners can govern and protect their customers just as safely if not better than some of the bigger conglomerates . . . Remember small business owners like me have so much on the hook; ie. rent, payroll, and income for our sustainability; not to mention supporting our faith-based communities and our communities at large.

Let's consider the what impact on some of our black owned businesses such as barbers, small law firms, small retail stores, etc. who might have five or six customers a day one at a time. So, this is why, with a strong prayer for safety and wisdom, I stand with Governor Kemp's decision to shoulder and share the responsibility with the people; letting us work together to do what's right for our communities while keeping our families, our places of worship, customers and employees safe as well in these times of transition.

My colleague Sharon LeVell, COO of Dunwoody Diamonds USA & LeVell Properties agrees. Sharon is an African-American woman who has been running a company for over 25 years. She is in sync with the governor's plan, "I support Governor Kemp's decision on allowing the small businesses to take charge and make good and safe decisions for employees and their customers."

While the first round of health, safety and economics have been horrendous, catching the general public off guard, President Trump, supportive governors, houses of faith and valiant instant responders are leading the charge.

We are winning, thank God.

There are many concerns that must be answered.

Below is a link to a very lengthy composite of concerns from my collective.

Many of these concerns are voiced by some of whom are healthcare workers, business owners, educators, law enforcement officers, pastors and public servants. Many are overwhelmingly sad at the level of fear and distrust that everyone seems to have towards the government's ability to keep us safe right now. This goes beyond party lines and people really see this pandemic as a matter of life and death. While everyone seems to understand that the government has a heavy burden to weigh the safety of our citizens and the stability of our economy, we all feel like there is a lack of transparency when it comes to decision making that affects our most sensitive members of the population.

CDC data shows Covid-19 is affecting African Americans at exceptionally high rates.

The coronavirus pandemic is amplifying preexisting social inequities tied to race, class, and access to the health care system.

Why would the governor reopen businesses that benefit mostly from the black economy?

Why reopen when there is still a national shortage of PPE, hospital beds, and meds?

Also, what message are we sending to GA students about education and health when schools are closed, and children cannot participate in graduation or promotions, but aestiticians can perform bikini waxes and fitness enthusiasts can work out at Orange Theory or Pure Barre in close quarters.

What plans do you have to prevent crime and mischief when schools will be closed for five months instead of two and children will lack supervision?

If cases spike, what work options will be available for teachers with compromised immune systems if schools reopen in the fall?

Why are we reopening when we are still seeing new cases daily? How can we flatten the curve when chances for exposure will increase once the shelter in place order ends?

We are not prepared to address a spike in cases.

Many AA living conditions include elderly, infants and all in between living in close proximity. So, if a young adult member of the household has the virus, s/he is likely to spread it to the elder and/or infant because they are sharing an area of 1,200 sq ft.

I think there should be some guidelines/best practices communicated for uniformity. This is a new experience for all. Some church leadership, small business owners, etc, don't have the knowledge to execute a "safe" reopening. And how do we know what's working or what's not if every business/church is doing something different

Concern:

If Epidemiologists and other doctors continue to say, "Stay at home, to stay healthy!"

Then why would you (Governor) go against medical experts' recommendations?

How do you support your decision, medically? Please explain your rationale in regard to public health.

Bottom line: Where is the medical data to support your expedited decision to reopen businesses so soon?

Why Trump?

Concerns:

1. Why did the Governor make moves to reopen before his initial April 30th date?
2. An increase of cases will happen and the need for more PPE
3. Unknown effect on children in the future
4. Shortage of masks & gowns at the VA Hospital
5. Has the governor stepped foot in the hotspots of GA and/or interviewed medical personnel at that hospital
6. How can you ensure the safety of the business owners
7. Will there be uniformity in guidelines for ALL businesses
8. Healthcare workers will continue to be overextended and exposed to possibly becoming infected

What People Would Like to See Before Reopening the State:

1. Continue to shelter in place unless people exercise high levels of caution (masks, PPE etc)
2. Bell curve should decrease before reopening the state
3. More testing sites and rapid testing (in Dekalb, only 84 tests can be performed daily)
4. Mandates of specific safety measures (people will not be comfortable going back on the economy without proper and adequate safety measures)

5. The elderly population needs extra precaution. Assisted Living facilities need to continue their same guidelines, but how can we ensure the facility workers are being safe after businesses reopen? They can then venture out and become infected and possibly infect residents.

This is actually a brief list and we feel like the government needs a more inclusive approach before reopening. We don't feel prepared to reopen and don't share the ability to look at numbers when we actually know names and faces of victims. One life is one too many to die unnecessarily. We want the state to reopen, we just need more structure to support it.

Interestingly, many of these concerns are already being addressed. Sadly, many are so angry and scared, they won't ever find out how much is really being done. Answers are available at whitehouse.gov links. We are winning.

POTUS GUIDELINES

COVID-19 Faith Community Resources

—COVID-19 Recommended Preventive Practices and FAQs for Faith-based and Community Leaders

—Considering Faith, Community, and Mental Health During the COVID-19 Crisis

The Paycheck Protection Plan

The Paycheck Protection Program prioritizes millions of Americans employed by small businesses and eligible nonprofits by authorizing up to $349 billion toward job retention and certain other expenses. Last week, the Administration issued a FAQ Regarding Participation of Faith-Based Organizations in PPP and EIDL, which clarifies how the affiliation provision impacts faith-based entities.

—Paycheck Protection Program Loans: Frequently Asked Questions (*Updated April 14*)

—Top-line overview of the paycheck protection loan program

—More information for borrowers

—Borrower Application Form – (*Updated April 2)*

—Interim Final Rule

—Interim Final Rule on Affiliation

• Interim Final Rule – Additional Eligibility Criteria and Requirements for Certain Pledges of Loans – (*Posted April 14)*

—Applicable Affiliation Rules

—Find an eligible lender

—Lender Assistance Hotline: (833) 572-0502

For more information and updates, visit **Treasury.gov/CARES** and **SBA.gov/PayCheckProtection.**

Assistance for American Workers and Families:

—Assistance for American Workers and Families

—Preserving Jobs for American Industry

How to Help – If you or your organization are interested in helping the effort to combat the spread of COVID-19, FEMA has established a website with more information. Examples for the private sector include:

- **To sell medical supplies or equipment** to the federal government, please submit a price quote under the COVID-19 PPE and Medical Supplies Request for Quotation. Full details can be found in the solicitation (Notice ID 70FA2020R00000011).
- This solicitation requires registration with the System for Award Management (SAM) in order to be considered for award, pursuant to applicable regulations and guidelines. Registration information can be found at www.sam.gov. Registration must be "ACTIVE" at the time of award.
- If you have medical supplies or equipment to donate, please provide us details on what you are offering.
- If you are a hospital or healthcare provider in need of medical supplies, please contact your state, local, tribal or territory department of public health and/or emergency management agency.
- If you are interested in doing business with FEMA and supporting the response to COVID-19 with your company's non-medical goods and/or services, please submit your inquiry to the Department

of Homeland Security (DHS) Procurement Action Innovative Response Team (PAIR) team at DHSIndustryLiaison@hq.dhs.gov.

• For all other issues and concerns not related to offering products, services, or donations, please e-mail nbeoc@max.gov.

For additional information please visit FEMA's Website:

30 Days to Slow the Spread

President Trump announced updated guidelines to continue slowing the spread of Coronavirus in America. This 30-day window will be crucial: If every American does his or her part, the latest model suggests we could save 1 million or more U.S. lives. Please click here for more information: 30 Days to Slow the Spread (Español)

If you are a healthcare worker and would like to volunteer to assist in New York City, please find more information here.

The Administration for Children and Families to Release Funding to Support the Child Care and Development Block Grant. More on the HHS Website.

"President Trump has secured more than $6 billion in funding to help meet the needs of America's most vulnerable during this time of crisis, including those who need assistance affording child care," said HHS Secretary Alex Azar. "As part of the President's all-of-America approach to combating the coronavirus, ACF is providing extra support for human services that Americans—including healthcare workers, first responders, and other essential workers—may rely on even more in this time of crisis."

FEMA Announces Funding Notice for Emergency Management Performance Grant Supplemental Allocation. See More Here.

The Department of Homeland Security and FEMA are announcing the funding notice for an additional $100 million in supplemental Emergency Management Performance Grant Program funds. The money is available to all 50 states and six territories as part of the Coronavirus Aid, Relief, and Economic Security (CARES) Act. All applications must be submitted by April 28.

EPA Continues Efforts to Increase the Availability of Disinfectant Products for Use Against the Novel Coronavirus. Read More.

"There is no higher priority for the Trump Administration than protecting the health and safety of Americans," said Assistant Administrator for the Office of Chemical Safety and Pollution Prevention Alexandra Dapolito Dunn. "EPA recognizes the important role the agency plays in protecting public health and the environment and ensuring that Americans continue to have access to effective and approved disinfectants that can help combat the spread of COVID-19. The flexibilities that we are providing in today's temporary policy change will help ensure Americans have access to the products they need to protect their families during this public health emergency."

Why Trump?

IRS, Security Summit Partners Warn Tax Professionals on Scams, Urge Additional Security Measures to Protect Taxpayer Data. Read the Details.

The IRS, state tax agencies and the nation's tax industry continue to see an upswing in data thefts from tax professionals as cybercriminals try to take advantage of COVID-19 and Economic Impact Payments to create new scams.

Federal Banking Agencies to Defer Appraisals and Evaluations for Real Estate Transactions Affected by COVID-19. For More Information.

The federal banking agencies today issued an interim final rule to temporarily defer real estate-related appraisals and evaluations under the agencies' interagency appraisal regulations. The Federal Reserve Board, the Federal Deposit Insurance Corporation, and the Office of the Comptroller of the Currency are providing this temporary relief to allow regulated institutions to extend financing to creditworthy households and businesses quickly in the wake of the national emergency declared in connection with COVID-19.

For the most up-to-date information, please see the CDC's Website.

Lastly, we have attached a document on Considering Faith, Community, and Mental Health During the COVID-19 Crisis. The document is attached as a pdf and you can share the document by clicking here.

Why Trump?

Direct *links* to the following temporary programs (or temporary expansions of current programs) are below (including application forms):

Paycheck Protection Program (PPP):

https://www.sba.gov/fundingprograms/loans/corona
virus-relief-options/paycheck-protection-program-
ppp

Economic Injury Disaster Loan (EIDL) Emergency Advance:

https://www.sba.gov/fundingprograms/loans/corona
virus-relief-options/economic-injury-disaster-loan-
emergency-advance

SBA Express Bridge Loans:

https://www.sba.gov/fundingprograms/loans/corona
virus-relief-options/sba-express-bridge-loans

SBA Debt Relief:

https://www.sba.gov/funding-
programs/loans/coronavirus-relief-options/sba-debt-
relief

And for those folks following the Interim Final Rule (IFR) for the PPP above (with respect to religious liberty issues, etc.)

Link: **(https://washex.am/3iWeUnt)**

President Trump continues to mobilize supplies to the frontlines to protect our healthcare workers and combat the coronavirus.

Why Trump?

· Personal Protective Equipment (PPE) deliveries coordinated or currently being shipped by FEMA and HHS:

- 38.2 million N95 respirators
- 2.6 million surgical masks
- 5.5 million face shields
- 4.7 million surgical gowns
- 30.3 million gloves
- 212,000 coveralls
- 8,600 medical station beds

Ventilators provided or shipped so far from the Strategic National Stockpile and the Department of Defense:

More than 10,800 nationwide.

- 4,400 to New York
- 1,558 to New Jersey
- 700 to Michigan
- 600 to Illinois
- 470 to Maryland
- 400 to Louisiana

FEMA launched Project Air Bridge to expedite imports of critical PPEs.

More than 40 Air Bridge flights have taken place as of April 14.

28 million tablets of *hydroxychloroquine* have been shipped across the country from the Strategic National Stockpile.

Why Trump?

"I urge you, first of all, to pray for all people. Ask God to help them; intercede on their behalf, and give thanks for them. Pray this way for kings and all who are in authority so that we can live peaceful and quiet lives marked by godliness and dignity," 1 Timothy 2:1-2 NLT.

Also, miraculously, as rescue funds and supplies are depleted, yet soon to be replenished funds. We continue to thank God for blessing our president of the United States, Donald John Trump — and all leaders for strength and wisdom.

Please pray, *stay safe and God bless you.*

Why Trump?

Friday, 17 Apr 2020 12:03 PM

We see, realize and celebrate our ethnic uniqueness and distinctions. God is merciful, loving us all.

In a recent announcement President Donald John Trump expressed concern and promises hope for America's Black community. He is praying for and listen to black and brown voices.

Why are blacks at high risk from COVID-19? A threefold reason; intentional targeting from the population control community, dependency on human systems rather than God, and lack of knowledge.

"But when Moses delivered this message to the Israelites, they didn't even hear him — they were that beaten down in spirit by the harsh slave conditions." — Exodus 6:9 MSG

We, as black and brown Americans, are often in a position of not receiving certain life affirming resources because we are lacking the knowledge required to access them.

"My people are destroyed for lack of knowledge: because thou hast rejected knowledge, I will also reject thee, that thou shalt be no priest to me: seeing thou hast forgotten the law of thy God, I will also forget thy children." — Hosea 4:6 KJV

As a 70-year-old African-American woman, I am very interested in what is going on in America and around the world today; and not just in the Black community.

Why Trump?

Consider this; religion, philosophy and science agree that the concept of separate human races is socially engineered.

We are one blood, one human race. (Acts 17:26-28)

"We all bleed the same." President Donald John Trump

Over the last several hours I have received urgent messages and questions from colleagues. One of the messages is that black businesses are being denied COVID-19 CARES Act funding by banks. Another message explained that submitting an application is a barrier in the qualifications which requires reading comprehension to qualification requirements that are unreasonable for target market. Lack of education; someone needs to do a webinar for us.

I couldn't agree more with the webinar route.

I'm involved in several such sessions.

In fact, as an adviser to Black Voices for Trump, I participate in offering information and training sessions. Also, there are local banks and SBA officials that can help applicants. The challenge is, if some of these sources or any leaders seem connected or favorable towards the current POTUS administration, they become suspect, enemies to those in need.

One very necessary approach is to continue enlarging the diversity of ethnic communities that are praying for and advising our leaders. While the Trump administration has done more for the Black community than previous administrations have done in decades, we are praying that this trajectory continues to soar.

The new advisory group on reopening the economy is a good example. When included, small business advisors can help with insight on diversity, and help to navigate the 30,000,000 plus small businesses, many of which are owned by Black and Brown entrepreneurs.

While some people may not agree with the sources of viable information, may I remind you; please don't shoot the messenger.

There are serious questions abroad for which we must seek answers. For instance, why, in the Black community, are there such high mortality rates for abortion, hypertension, diabetes, breast cancer, and other human conditions?

Again — There is a threefold reason; intentional targeting from the population control community, dependency on human systems rather than God, and lack of knowledge. Please people, wake up and connect the dots! We are dealing with a three-headed monster.

Blacks are often suspicious of sources that have been maligned by swamp creatures. For example, ask wary Blacks to visit www.whitehouse.gov and they may say "No."

Instead of visiting the site they automatic assumed, "That's Trump! You can't trust him! He's a racist!" This type of reaction fodders "lack of knowledge."

Why Trump?

Some news outlets even refuse to air daily updates, an act which denies the public access to necessary information. For example, today, April 16, 2020, some news sources are broadcasting that the COVID-19 CARES Act are depleted, without including the truth that more help is on the way. We must learn to examine information from multiple sources. Lack of knowledge is a common enemy.

"We must learn to live together as brothers [and sisters], or perish together as fools." – Prophet Martin Luther King, Jr.

My friends, wherever we live in the world, for me living here in America, where "In God We Trust," we are one human race. We are not colorblind.

We see, realize and celebrate our ethnic uniqueness and distinctions. God is merciful, loving us all.

"Pray diligently. Stay alert, with your eyes wide open in gratitude. Don't forget to pray for us." – Colossians 4:2 MSG

Unbelievably, on a call with Black Voices for Trump today, Keenan Williams, Trump Texas field organizer, shared his spiritual redemption testimony. Remarkably, his spiritual awakening coincided with his world view. He spoke of having been a Democrat and is now supporting President Trump. Suddenly, on the webinar, messages deriding him with profanity for making his transition popped up. Again, they are ignoring the life affirming message, despising the messenger. However, Keenan correctly advises us to share truth with intent to liberate, not to argue.

Why Trump?

"You can't win if you offend." —Keenan Williams, Texas field organizer.

"Have I therefore become your enemy, because I tell you the truth?" – Galatians 4:16 KJV

We must pray and move ahead preaching, teaching, and proclaiming truth.

"My people are being destroyed because they don't know me. Since you priests refuse to know me, I refuse to recognize you as my priests. Since you have forgotten the laws of your God, I will forget to bless your children." — Hosea 4:6 NLT

Tuesday, 14 Apr 2020 4:55 PM

With all too many of the news and daily reports filled with fear and terror regarding COVID-19, I don't know about you, but I believe that it is time to exercise faith over fear. We must join President Trump; we must pray rather than panic.

"We must learn to live together as brothers [and sisters], or perish together as fools." — Prophet, the Rev. Dr. Martin Luther King, Jr.

As to conspiracy theories? Some of them we can take with a grain of salt. Others? There is some truth out there. When I prayed and asked God: 'Is this you causing Covid-19?' surprisingly the answer was in Psalm 2.

"Why are the nations so angry? Why do they waste their time with futile plans? The kings of the earth prepare for battle; the rulers plot together against the Lord and against his anointed one. 'Let us break their chains,' they cry, 'and free ourselves from slavery to God.' But the one who rules in heaven laughs. The Lord scoffs at them. For the Lord declares, 'I have placed my chosen king on the throne in Jerusalem, on my holy mountain.'" – Psalms 2:1-4, 6 NLT

Wow! God did not dump COVID-19 on us? So why does God allow this?

GOD wants us to seek Heaven for answers.

"Then if my people who are called by my name will humble themselves and pray and seek my face and turn from their wicked ways, I will hear from heaven

and will forgive their sins and restore their land." 2 Chronicles 7:14

"We don't worship government, we worship God." – President Donald J. Trump.

Yes. Catastrophes are as old as sin. Solutions come from God, not humans. It's very important during these troublesome days to have physical, soulful, and spiritual balance.

For example, my uncle Prophet the Rev. Dr. Martin Luther King, Jr., said that science gives us facts, religion gives us morals; the two are not rivals. I agree; which is why I emphasize that medicine, safety and nourishment of the physical body and nourishment of the soul and spirit are all essential services.

On Easter Sunday, my pastor Theo McNair, spiritual leader of Believers Bible Christian Church taught us that Jesus is the answer to all of humanity's problems.

I worshipped God on Facebook last Sunday.

However, I am also grateful for the intervention strategies that are available www.whitehouse.gov. We must continue to seek God for strategies to overcome this enemy COVID-19.

While we are participating in the 30 days to slow the virus from home or wherever we are, we must pray, assist others, support life, and avoid fear and panic. We must seek facts, and apply faith rather than fear.

Why Trump?

I have included five links below for your consideration. As you review and/or study, please pray and use discernment.

"But when Moses delivered this message to the Israelites, they didn't even hear him—they were that beaten down in spirit by the harsh slave conditions." – Exodus 6:9 MSG

Finally, as you consider these five links and information therein, please remember to pray. Issues of separate races and separate classes are socially engineered by humans.

"Have I now become your enemy because I am telling you the truth?" — Galatians 4:16 NLT

There are no separate human races. We are not colorblind.

We can see God's beauty in every culture. As human beings, we are of various ethnic nations, tongues and tribes, we are the human family. We are one human race, one blood. (Acts 17:26-28)

"We all bleed the same." — U.S. President Donald J. Trump

My friends, we need God's help. We need each other.

Remember, we do not need to panic. God loves us. We need to pray; we need to avoid fear and instead we need to exercise faith. Remember, above all things, God is agape love and His wisdom is with us.

Why Trump?

Tuesday, 03 Mar 2020 9:51 AM

When peripherals collide, convergence is imminent: Reflections as 2020 Black History Month comes to an end last week.

Sitting across from President Donald John Trump during a landmark historic round table black history discussion, I smiled as he asked the group gathered whether we would like to be called "Black" or "African Americans?"

(Official White House Photo by Tia Dufour)

As one, we resounded, "Black!" As a group, we went on to explain that while the reasons are complicated, the terms are acceptably interchangeable.

What was most compelling about the honor of sitting with the president of the United States and powerful and motivated peers was the air of transparency in the room. President Trump is an active listener and a consummate communicator. The atmosphere was charged with hope and vision; not racist, not colorblind.

Our ethnicity was there in the White House, for all to *see*.

"Pray diligently. Stay alert, with your eyes wide open in gratitude." — Colossians 4:2 (MSG).

"We all bleed the same." — President Donald J. Trump

With America's "Black History Month" now behind us, over the moon and back would describe the Black History events that occurred during the 29 days of Black History Month 2020. Presidential pardons, clemency, fair housing seminars, round table talks and more mark this landmark leap year. With President Trump, our most prolife president ever, at the helm, there are even brighter days ahead — especially for our babies in the womb.

"We don't worship government, we worship God." — President Donald J. Trump

(Official White House Photo by Tia Dufour)

Why Trump?

Thursday, after the round table discussion with black leaders, President Trump, joined by first lady Melania Trump, spoke at a jam packed White House reception honoring African American History Month.

The celebration this year coincides with the 150th anniversary of the 15th Amendment.

POTUS noted that throughout America's journey, African Americans have enhanced — and advanced — every aspect of American life. "Their fight for equality, representation, and respect motivates us to continue working for a more promising, peaceful, and hopeful future for every American," notes President Trump in his 2020 National African American History Month Proclamation:

"Set this year apart as holy, a time to proclaim freedom throughout the land for all who live there. It will be a jubilee year for you, when each of you may return to the land that belonged to your ancestors and return to your own clan."– Leviticus 25:10 (NLT).

As one who part of boots on the ground along with my goddaughter Angela Stanton-King and mentor Bruce LeVell, I am honored to have had the opportunity during Black History Month, to pray with our president, to hear his heart for the success of America, and to encourage and celebrate all the "promises made and promises kept" by President Donald John Trump.

Why Trump?

(Official White House Photo by Tia Dufour)

Our movement today.

As I write this message, I'm on my way to Washington, D.C. with Angela Stanton-King to join others for a special African American History observance at the White House.

It's also Leap Year. So, as I go, I pray for "a leap of faith."

Just a few hours ago, I was in the Georgia Mountains at a prayer breakfast. In D.C., along with the acknowledgement of Black History, we will be praying and networking.

President Trump has said, "We don't worship government. We worship God."

Why Trump?

When peripherals collide, convergence is imminent.

It's no coincidence that this leap year we find ourselves on a precipice overlooking a quagmire of American controversy in many areas of life; spiritual, emotional, financial, social and political.

There are so many soft edges, unclear murky gray and smeared boundary lines.

It is during times like these, prayer and reflection are appropriate.

This year, I'm praying that America will do three things:

1. Repent for our sins and turn to God.
2. Embrace the sanctity of all human life.
3. Reject the socially engineered concept of separate races and the socially engineered lies and divisive scars of racism.

We are all *one human race*. Our skin color does not define our race; our One Blood does. We may be different ethnicities; our skin color may be different hues; our cultures may be different. But we are still just *one race, human*. "Racism," "racial tension," 'interracial,' "race relations," and the like are all human constructs serving to divide us.

This socially engineered system defies religion, science, and biology.

It's a macabre construct of separate races promulgating the lie of racism; the lie that we humans are of different races.

Why Trump?

This is a lie that the enemy has been spreading for decades *and* centuries. We need to change our whole perspective and way of thinking and see each other as God sees us, as valuable, living children of God created in his image— and as one human family.

"We must learn to live together as brothers [and sisters], or perish together as fools." – The Rev. Dr. Martin Luther King, Jr.

February is Black History Month in America.

This national observance was established by noted American historian Carter Godwin Woodson. As a respected author, journalist and the founder of the Association for the Study of African American Life and History, he was one of the first scholars to study African-American history.

Dr. Woodson was the second African American to receive a doctorate from Harvard University. He dedicated his career to the field of African-American history and lobbied extensively to establish Black History Month as a nationwide institution, with the hopes that black Americans would one day be fully embraced in America's historical accounts — not separately, but inclusively.

This year, African Americans have new reasons to celebrate, and many are saluting President Trump for measurable gains in our black communities.

Thus, we are grateful.

Leaping ahead through all that 2020 will bring, let's pray for America, holding on to love and truth.

Why Trump?

Monday, 05 October 2020 10:20 AM

Across America and around the world, many are praying for President Donald Trump and first lady Melania Trump as they battle COVID-19. My prayers are added, with the hope that God will redeem us all from the deadly plague.

As one who has been blessed to pray for and with the Trump administration, I'm honored to release my memoirs about the journey at this time.

For four years, I've been answering a question that has become a joy and a burden; depending on who's asking. Why Trump? In my latest memoir, I share a lesson I learned at the feet of my granddaddy Martin Luther King, Sr. who was affectionately known to the world as "Daddy King" to explain the often-asked question, "Why do you support Donald Trump?"

In 1960, Granddaddy made a difficult decision to leave his loyalty to his Baptist Faith and the Republican Party to vote for John Kennedy, a Catholic Democrat. Granddaddy voted for JFK who helped to rescue Uncle MLK from danger.

During the 2016 presidential race Donald John Trump was one of my top five candidate preferences. In 2020 it is easy for me to answer the question, "Why Trump?" Over the last four years, I have had a front row seat watching President Trump fight for religious liberties not only here in America, but around the globe. I have watched him champion the rights of the unborn. I have watched him advance opportunities in Black America.

With POTUS I've taken a page from my Granddaddy's journal. I've put faith and expediency over church denomination and politics. Donald J. Trump is my president. I've got my vote, and my prayers. Both are in favor of President Trump and his "promises made and promises kept."

Again, let's pray for healing and better days ahead.

Why Trump?

Friday, 07 February 2020 02:20 PM

This week President Donald J. Trump's SOTU address glorified God, encouraged America, and gave honor to whom honor is due.

The next day, the National Prayer Services activities kicked off.

At the nation's 68th National Prayer Breakfast, yesterday.

The president was joined by over 3,500 participants.

President Trump, U.S. House Speaker Rep. Nancy Pelosi, D-Calif., and others spoke.

CeCe Winans sang. The bipartisan Congressional Prayer Caucus (who hosted the event) opened with worship music and prayers.

In the keynote address, conservative author Arthur Brooks encouraged biblical love amid a nationwide "crisis of contempt and polarization," reminding attendees that Jesus ordered his followers to love — not just tolerate — enemies.

Afterward, in a moment of heart-wrenching transparency, President Trump revealed the challenges of embracing agape love, by declaring "I'm trying."

For a brief political hiatus, all were prayerful. What a blessing.

Why Trump?

My February week of prayer in Washington, D.C. ended at The Museum of The Bible with a delightful and uplifting oasis experience at An Evening to Inspire," an event taking place in the midst of this phenomenal week. Pray for America everyone.

Amidst skipped handshakes and emotional speech rip-ups, America experienced a week of prayer; spearheaded by non-other than our nation's 45th president.

To be honest, while President Trump chose to avoid shaking hands with his adversaries during the week of the impeachment saga, I must admit that I agree with his wisdom.

There is actually scripture covering that:

"Lay hands suddenly on no man, neither be partaker of other men's sins: keep thyself pure." (1 Timothy 5:22)

The year 2020 is indeed off to a prayerful beginning.

Let us not forget that in January of this year, President Trump, our most prolife president ever, granted us a historical first by speaking to a large audience at The March for Life.

Meanwhile, as Valentine's Day approaches, Jensine Bard writes:

"It's time for respite as we approach a day that is marked by love — Valentine's Day and a movie that will take you there!!!"

"First Lady," is a story of firsts — "in love, in romance and, yes, politics too," according to Jensine Bard. It features a stellar cast: Nancy Stafford, Corbin Bernsen, Stacey Dash, Dr. Alveda C King, and a cameo by the film's writer and director: Nina May — just to name a few.

Anticipated release in selected theaters nationwide Valentine's Day Feb. 14, 2020.

Yes, 2020 is progressing. In the coming days, may God have mercy on our souls.

May America repent, return to God, sow and reap agape love.

May America also receive the eternal blessings of victory in Christ Jesus.

Why Trump?

Friday, 08 November 2019 05:42 PM

I am in Atlanta today with President Trump and it's been a great day for the president.

There is a lot of support for Trump in Atlanta. We all need to love, forgive, and support our leaders. Through loving our enemies, we can all get along. We can have the greatest nation on the planet.

Today we rolled out the "Black Voices for Trump" coalition. There is a lot of energy and excitement in the air. President Trump spoke to a large crowd of supporters along with Vice President Mike Pence and Housing and Urban Development Secretary Ben Carson.

In his run for the presidency in 2016, in asking for the Black vote — "What do you have to lose?" Since that day, with many promises kept, POTUS has consistently shown us what we have to gain. Now, 3 years later, not only did Blacks not lose anything, but we have gained a lot with the unemployment rate being at historic lows and the establishment of opportunity zones to help revitalize struggling neighborhoods. He has also been the most prolife president we have ever had, protecting all life from the womb to the tomb. With Blacks accounting for about a third abortions, that's a lot of Black babies our president is protecting.

Why Trump?

So, please pray for us! God is good.

Here is my prayer I shared at the event.

Lift every voice and sing, till earth and heaven ring; ring with the harmony of liberty...

Father God you say in your word to pray for those in authority that we may live peaceful lives.

Today we thank you for President Donald J. Trump. We thank you that he is Pro-God, leading us to understand that as human beings, we are a family of one blood. We all bleed the same. We thank you for the beauty of ethnicity, of skin color, not to divide us, but to unite us. We are not colorblind. We celebrate diversity.

Lord, we thank you for President Trump; his promises made and promises kept. Please continue to grant him your love, compassion, courage and wisdom. Bless him, his family, his administration, his supporters, and yes, his enemies.

Finally, Lord forgive us our sins, heal us from within and without, from womb to tomb. God bless humanity and America with four more years with Donald J. Trump in your hands as our president.

For thine is the Kingdom, and the Power and the glory, forever. Amen.

Why Trump?

Tuesday, 10 September 2019 11:00 AM

This week, President Trump is still keeping his word to Historically Black Colleges and Universities (HBCUs). He's slated to speak at the HBCU Conference today, where he is expected to unveil recent advances in his successful strategies.

Meanwhile, as Executive Director of Civil Rights for The Unborn for Priests for Life, Evangelist Alveda King, your "boots on the ground" freedom fighter, is joining pro-life activists Rev. Frank Pavone, Janet Morana, and other pro-life and Christian leaders from around the country in D.C. today to knock on Congress' doors to demand justice for womb babies.

I'm especially looking forward to visiting offices of members of The Congressional Black Caucus with news of our Black and Brown Treatise, which outlines strategies to ending crimes against humanity such as abortion, human trafficking, and racism. While I won't be attending the annual Congressional Black Caucus' annual summit this week, I will be praying for them.

This week's CBC events are sponsored by The Annual Legislative Conference. ALC is the Congressional Black Caucus Foundation's leading policy conference on issues impacting African Americans and the global black community; where Black and Brown elected officials join "thought" leaders, legislators, grassroots organizers, influencers, and celebrities annually.

Why Trump?

As fans gather to support CBCF's mission, network, and to engage in policy sessions and discussions, I have some questions. I can't help wondering how the CBC will tie in demands for impeachment, more tax-payer funding for abortion providers, and abortion as a means of population control, with a platform that will unite and strengthen America?

I also wonder how the CBC can continue to turn a blind eye to the Black on Black violence in our communities? How can they ignore the harm of race baiting while denying the truth; racism is a socially engineered evil that can be conquered by God's love? We are not colorblind.

We are one blood/one human race.

We are in a season of Jubilee, where as one blood, we can unite as one human race, and truly unite as "one nation under God here in America."

One example of this process is Criminal Justice Reform, an advance ignited by the iconic bipartisan First Step Act and Second Step Act.

Thankfully, we have a president that sees the color of the blood, as well as the color of our skin, as human characteristics that unite us rather than divide us.

For now, it's full speed ahead. God bless America and all of humanity; this week and forever.

Why Trump?

Thursday, 08 February 2018 11:10 AM

Starting with a new presidential appointment, Black History Month is full of surprises for 2018. President Donald J. Trump has honored one of my heroes, Frederick Douglass with the empowering of The Frederick Douglass Bicentennial Commission.

I'm blessed to serve America as a new member of this commission.

Moving forward, let's reflect on the president's campaign promises to address racism by ensuring us that "when we give everyone a great America; safety, security, a reason to belong, that will serve the issue."

The president also declared early on in his post as commander in chief, "No matter what color our skin is, we all bleed red." His insight into the one blood truth, coupled with his frequent reminders that, "We don't serve government, we serve God; in God we trust" are encouraging to say the least.

The month started off with the launch of my annual Black History Tour; this time from Titusville, Florida, which is the new home of Priests for Life. I'm director of Civil Rights for The Unborn for that organization. It was a blessing to visit local schools and the Titusville campus of Eastern Florida State College.

Meanwhile, the Congressional Black Caucus sat down on the job during President Trump's inspiring

State of the Union Address. The petulant actions of the majority of The CBC cripple the dreams of America. They must be addressed. Expect to hear more from activists for genuine social justice this month.

It was also a blessing to give a Black History shout out at the 2018 Rose Day Rally in Oklahoma City, Oklahoma.

It's also important to note that while we are one blood/one race (Acts, Chapter 17:26), the black/African/American community still celebrates a month of educating the masses regarding many notable contributions of blacks in the U.S. — that are unknown and undocumented in certain historical annals. These efforts are designed to unite us; never to divide us. Herein is a key to unlocking racial reconciliation.

There's been a flurry of discourse regarding the Dodge Ram commercial featuring the voice of the Rev. Dr. Martin Luther King, Jr. with community service as a theme. On a positive note, many are saying that the ad sparked them to find the entire Dr. King speech and listen to it. That's millennials for you; ever seeking truth. The line about "a heart to serve" with the ultrasound of the baby's heartbeat was definitely a kind of ram in the bush "Aha" moment.

Why Trump?

Coming up this month:

White House Black History Event

Launch of King Family Legacy Library at Millennium Gate Museum

Finally, please remember to pray for America, and watch out for "King Truths" and the upcoming Roe v. Wade movie.

Why Trump?

Thursday, 08 August 2019 12:16 PM

"Finally, brethren, whatsoever things are true, whatsoever things are honest, whatsoever things are just, whatsoever things are pure, whatsoever things are lovely, whatsoever things are of good report; if there be any virtue, and if there be any praise, think on these things." Philippians 4:8

Our hearts go out and our prayers go up for the victims in America's most recent tragedies.

Perhaps the most comforting compliment to President and First Lady Trump's outreach to the families of the victims of the recent massacres in Ohio and Texas is the appeal of a young boy who asks Americans to respond to the horrendous violence by performing 22 acts of kindness to those around us.

Meanwhile, in comparison, comments made by former Congressman Beto O'Rourke, and former Vice President Joe Biden, both accusing President Trump of being a white supremacist, are untimely and unseemly.

Biden and his compatriots are not being truthful.

There are instances where President Trump denounces White Supremacy.

Biden and his compatriots support immoral baby killers including Planned Parenthood and the abortion lobby.

Why Trump?

Race baiters fail to mention that George Wallace apologized. It was a reaching-out moment of reconciliation, of Wallace's asking for — and receiving — forgiveness. In a statement read for him — he was too ill to speak — Wallace told those in the crowd who had marched 30 years ago: "Much has transpired since those days. A great deal has been lost and a great deal gained, and here we are. My message to you today is, welcome to Montgomery. May your message be heard. May your lessons never be forgotten."

Fake News refuses to cover President Trump's accomplishments, including fighting for The Unborn, criminal justice reform, and aid to HBCUs (Historically Black Colleges and Universities). Meanwhile they ignore Biden's part in incarceration of hundreds of thousands of Blacks.

Shame on Biden and his compatriots. Race baiting while POTUS and FLOTUS pay respect to the grieving. PRAY FOR AMERICA.

"Be not overcome of evil, but overcome evil with good." Romans 12:21

Monday, 11 December 2017 05:29 PM

Amid protests and boycotts over his attendance during the opening of two civil rights museums in Jackson, Mississippi last week, our US President Donald John Trump said, "Martin Luther King, Jr. was a man I have studied, watched, and admired for my entire life."

As God would have it, I read the account of the president's visit to the new museums — from Rome, Italy — where yours truly has been invited to attend the Catholic-inspired non-governmental organizations' (NGO) conference during this Christmas season.

In the midst of the stress, strife and distractions the world can cook up, especially during the holidays, the blessing of combing prayers, work and Christmas cheer is appropriate and indescribable. Meanwhile, President Trump's words continue to be uplifting.

I'm considering this trip to Rome to be a Priests for Life working tour, one laced with holiday cheer. While here, I am remembering the words of Pope Francis, especially the section about the power of love to remain resilient, even in the face of trials. In his pastoral letter on the family, "Amoris Laetitia" the pope writes, "Here I think of the words of Martin Luther King who met every kind of trial and tribulation with fraternal love."

The pope also quotes at length my Uncle's 1957 sermon given at Montgomery, Alabama's Dexter Avenue Baptist Church, in which my uncle, Dr. King said, "The person who hates you most has some good in him; even the nation that hates you most has some good in it; even the race [Acts 17:26 One Blood/One Human Race] that hates you most has some good in it."

Then Pope Francis expounded further on Dr. King's words, "And when you come to the point that you look in the face of every [person] and see deep down within [that human being] what religion calls 'the image of God,' you begin to love [people] in spite of [everything]," Dr. King continued.

Needless to say, Dr. King's message is relevant to the purpose and mission of my Christmas tour. A tour which spreads the message of the agape love of Jesus Christ and the sanctity of life — globally.

Photos and social media accounts of this journey are forthcoming on Priests for Life on the Frontlines.

Notwithstanding the jet lag, the journey continues to be amazing. Along with visits to the Vatican, and meeting leaders of the Christian world, there's also time for sightseeing such as St. Peter's Square, The Trevi Fountain and quaint sidewalk cafes.

An exceptional delight has been the fellowship with the people of the Italian community; such hospitality at every turn, regardless of ethnicity, religion and socio-economic conditions.

A special interview and visit to the home of EWTN's host of "Joan's Rome," Joan Lewis, has caused me to pause and make note of what I'm calling "GG's (Gorgeous Grandma's) Visit with Joan at her Home for the Holidays." I can only wish that you'd been able to join us for the warm and delicious coffee, cake, and historical perusing among Joan's collection of beautiful memories — expressed in so many ways that lovely morning.

Since my blogs are usually filled with lectures, lessons, encouragement and prayers for concerns for the world, it's a refreshing change of pace to share some joyful highlights.

However, there's still some of the lecture mode going on during this journey as well. For instance, back home in America once again members of The Congressional Black Caucus and a few members of the "old guard 20th century civil rights movement" missed yet another opportunity to speak up for the civil rights of the unborn last Friday. They chose instead to boycott the opening of the two new civil rights museums in Mississippi. It is there President Trump visited to bless the historical site.

(Author's Note: In a 1958 interview, MLK expressed his view that neither party was perfect, saying, "I don't think the Republican Party is a party full of the almighty God nor is the Democratic Party. They both have weaknesses ... And I'm not inextricably bound to either party." MLK was never registered as Democrat or Republican. He was an Independent.)

Enough said about that for now; except that it's all part of the "work" angle of my Rome mission; to bring awareness of the sanctity of life issues to light.

Meanwhile, God's infinite love and mercy are allowing my heart to pray for you my beloved readers during this season, and to bring reconciliation to our broken communities.

As you join in by reading about my journaled Rome trek, and the soon to be released "King Truths," if you are hurting in any way, maybe from loss of a loved one or some other painful situation, may God's grace and goodness touch you during your deepest moments and bring light, love and healing to you!

There's more to come from Rome before we head for Home. Merry Christmas. Stay tuned. Ciao.

Monday, November 5, 2018, 11:05 AM

Have you voted yet? If so, I pray you voted for prolife candidates. If not, as an American citizen, don't miss out on exercising your Civil Right to vote. Many people marched and risked our lives for this freedom to cast our votes.

So, if you haven't done so yet, please go to the polls tomorrow and vote prolife. Life is our first Civil Right. A vote for Life strikes a blow to injustice.

A praying America is a greater America.

A working America is a greater America.

A safe and secure America is a greater America.

A just America is greater America.

Vote prolife.

Why vote prolife? With one punch of the ballot, one pull of the lever, one clicks of the mouse, one stroke of a pen; however, they do it at your poll; you strike a blow at that three-headed monster. We are all one blood/one human race. (Acts 17:26-28)

We must fight and vote for freedom for everyone; for the womb to the tomb.

Did you know that abortion, racism, human trafficking, and poverty are all part of the same dirty system? They are part of the three-headed swamp monster that's going down MAGA's drain.

God's people perish for lack of knowledge. Know your rights!

Martin Luther King, Jr. once demanded: "Give us the ballot!" Before his death, my beloved mentor, Pastor Allen McNair said: "Don't Vote for Sin!"

Whatever the outcome tomorrow, do your part. Vote for Life and Pray for America.

Make your vote count. Vote prolife.

Favorite Memes Collection

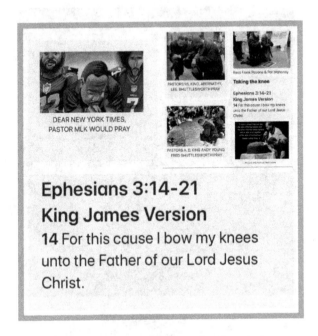

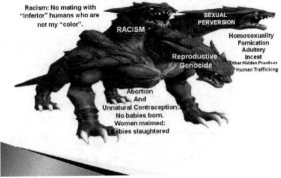

Why Trump?

"While we are protecting our history, we are overcoming our biases; this is happening simultaneously. There is no need to vandalize property and real estate in this process. We must remember the good; that's legacy. We must avoid repeating the bad; bad is sin. Remember, statues can be idols. As one blood, one human race; it's time to return to God. #GODPOWER"
Evangelist Alveda C. King

Why Trump?

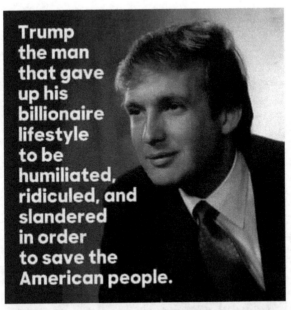

Trump the man that gave up his billionaire lifestyle to be humiliated, ridiculed, and slandered in order to save the American people.

Donald Trump

Artist 'astounded' to see his Trump painting hung in the White House

Epilogue

"(To the chief Musician upon Shoshannim, for the sons of Korah; Maschil, A Song of loves.) My heart is inditing a good matter: I speak of the things which I have made touching the king: my tongue is the pen of a ready writer." Psalm 45:1

It has been said that a picture is worth a thousand words which is why this book is mostly a cross between a journal and a scrapbook. This is the first time I have shared a substantial number of photos of my "Trump Journey." I share not to be boastful. I share because I have been blessed to share this road less traveled with some wonderfully blessed companions. We have laughed, cried and prayed together; and you will share that journey here.

This book is being released just prior to the U. S. 2020 elections. Only God knows what the short and long-term future holds. I'd like to believe that if my grandfather were here, he would understand why I have chosen to depart from tradition and supported President Trump. It has been said that the apple doesn't fall far from the tree.

Why Trump?

Sixty years ago, my grandfather Rev. Martin Luther King, Sr. used a "suitcase" of votes to redirect the establishment and transform a nation. All these years later, with faith in God, hope that God will bless America, and love for the human race, I cast my vote for life, liberty, the pursuit of happiness; and for Donald J. Trump

Being prolific in nature, and often even verbose, as a "Creative Evangelist," I have written many books, poems, songs, film scripts, plays and missives including op-eds and news reports. I have also been known to pick up a sketch pad here and there. Consequently, I have gained many monikers along the way, including that of "Scribe" and "Ready Writer" along this journey of life. My parents and grandparents taught me that with God, nothing is too hard or impossible. When I was a little girl, they invited me to dream, and encouraged my penchant for justice and love for humanity. This book is yet another rung in the ladder they built for me.

WHY TRUMP? is my newest adventure. Thank you for your prayers and support. God bless you.